D1382326

THE RIGGER

OPERATING WITH THE SAS

JACK WILLIAMS

Pen & Sword
MILITARY

First published in Great Britain in 2001 by
Leo Cooper

Reprinted in 2015 by
Pen & Sword Military
an imprint of
Pen & Sword Books Ltd
47 Church Street
Barnsley
South Yorkshire
S70 2AS

ISBN 978 1 47383 130 8

A CIP catalogue record for this book is available from the British Library

Typeset in Ehrhardt by
Mac Style Ltd, Bridlington, East Yorkshire
Printed and bound in the UK by CPI Group (UK) Ltd,
Croydon, CRO 4YY

Pen & Sword Books Ltd incorporates the imprints of Pen & Sword
Archaeology, Atlas, Aviation, Battleground, Discovery, Family History,
History, Maritime, Military, Naval, Politics, Railways, Select, Transport, True
Crime, and Fiction, Frontline Books, Leo Cooper, Praetorian Press, Seaforth
Publishing and Wharncliffe.

For a complete list of Pen & Sword titles please contact
PEN & SWORD BOOKS LIMITED
47 Church Street, Barnsley, South Yorkshire, S70 2AS, England
E-mail: enquiries@pen-and-sword.co.uk
Website: www.pen-and-sword.co.uk

CONTENTS

PROLOGUE

My first memory of life was running home across a narrow street called Tatton. Holding my left hand out in front of me and crying. I had banged on the front door with my right hand and waited, in pain, and wished my Mum would hurry up.

'What's the matter?' she asked.

I thrust my left hand forward for her to inspect it and between sobs said,

'I won all their marbles, so they put my little finger on a brick and hit it with another brick'.

I offered my left hand for sympathy and got it. Mum gave me a great big cuddle and with my head buried between her hips, I sobbed even more. My injury was too small to waste time on a hospital visit. Dad was working all the hours he could, and Mum was busy raising three children and working. My little finger would remain bent. The rest of my life seems to have been spent with my body being punctured by stitches and my bones being reset in plaster.

I was eight years old when our family really moved up in the world. Tatton Street was being demolished to make way for a new bus station and my Dad applied for a new council house, and got one. The new house was a three-bedroom semi with a loo inside. Sheer luxury! The only thing that remained the same was the toilet paper, yesterday's newspaper torn into convenient squares.

Junior school slipped past in my life and with it, my first recollections of the opposite sex. Yes, I found girls very attractive. Yes, I was aroused when I was around them. Yes, I was excited when I thought of them. Why, I didn't know. I was selected to play for the school football team and one year we won a cup. Anyone would have thought it was the World Cup we were so overjoyed. The headmaster even bought the team members a small bottle of lemonade each. We looked upon this as a major feat, as we had never known a teacher to buy us anything before. From our point of view, teachers existed for the sole purpose of disciplining us and filling our heads with useless information.

Onto an all boys' secondary modern school where I was put in the 'A' stream, why I don't know, I hated school. I just wanted to get out into the big wide world and join the men, but I had to wait another four years for that to happen. In the meantime all my reports said, 'Can do better', 'Not applying himself'. Dad was really disappointed that I'd finished up in a secondary modern school. It should have been the grammar school for his son. He went absolutely bananas when he found out that I had gone roller-skating instead of taking my eleven plus entrance exam.

There was a wood near where we lived and our gang used to go there because someone had attached a rope to the branch of a tree. The tree grew on the top of what we perceived to be a cliff, and the rope swung out over the cliff. One of the gang members grabbed the rope, swung out over the drop and then swung back. He landed and threw the rope to me with a smug expression on his face. I stepped forward, let the rope swing out, then swing back, then I ran forward, grabbed the rope and swung out on it. The problem was that in my haste to swing out further than the previous boy I mistimed the jump and failed to grip the rope correctly. It was another trip to the hospital where I had both my broken wrists put in plaster and one in a sling. It was most embarrassing for a twelve-year old boy as I couldn't feed myself, and worst of all, I couldn't go to the toilet by myself. When it was time to go, I'd stand in front of the toilet and yell,

'Mum'.

Mum would come into the bathroom, unzip me, pull it out, hold it for me and then keep asking,

'Have you finished?'

Six weeks later the plaster was removed and I was out with the gang again. We were running down a hill and gravity was making us run faster than we had ever run before. We yelled, laughed and shouted to each other as the wind rushed through our hair and our bright red cheeks tingled. It was a joyous glorious moment, until I put my foot in a rabbit hole. My feelings went from total joy to total pain in one millisecond as my foot stayed where it was and my body carried on moving. Tears burst out and flooded down my face and my body was wrenched by huge sobs. The two-mile journey back home was the most painful physical journey I'd ever made. The hospital put my leg in plaster. Six weeks later my leg came out of plaster. Two weeks after that, it was put back in plaster. Seven times in plaster and eleven times in strapping! I visited the hospital so often that people thought I was a permanent member of staff. My brother and I shared the same bed and one thing he couldn't stand was the feel of plaster. The impish bit of me would come out and I would wait until he was asleep, then I'd hook the plastered leg over one of his legs. He would wake up screaming. On one of my later visits the doctor referred me to the orthopedic department. The orthopedic department was a strange experience for a twelve year old boy. Wheel chairs, artificial legs, artificial arms and crutches greeted me as I walked in. They took my shoe and extended the heel out to the left by a quarter of an inch and I never went over and stretched the ligaments in my ankle again.

Looking back, secondary modern wasn't all that bad. The school bully picked on me once too often and I beat him up, didn't realise I could do it until I tried. I'll never forget the chemistry teacher doing an experiment with limestone. He dropped a couple of chunks of it into a beaker full of water that was sat on a tripod over a Bunsen burner and said,

'I'm just popping out to the storeroom. When I come back, the water will be milky white'.

When he came back, the water was black as coal. I got caned for pouring ink into his experiment. The deputy head left his marks on my life, or should I say my body. We would visibility shake if any teacher couldn't cope with us and they referred us to the deputy head. The deputy head had the wickedest cane in the school. Deviant was a thin, strong, long cane with lots of spring in it and he must have spent hours choosing it. All it took was a flick of the wrist to bring tears to our eyes. Deviant (The teachers all had names for their canes) left four of his welts on me once, and I couldn't sit down for three days. I would keep disappearing into the toilet, put my hand down the back of my trousers and gently massage the four-raised semi circles lines that stretched across my bum. The deputy head was the best caner in town. You behaved for a while after a visit to him. There was no way I could tell my Dad, or I would have got a telling off and maybe grounded. Two teachers were stood in front of the class on our final day at school discussing how they had coped with us.

'I've caned everybody in this class,' boasted one of them.

'I think I have too,' said the other teacher scratching his head. He pondered for a minute then said,

'Is there anybody in this class I haven't caned?'

George Dimlow was his name. George was someone who was outgrowing his strength. He was tall, willowy and white. He was a quiet intellectual that wore glasses and was completely out of place in this environment. He should have been at grammar school.

"You haven't caned me Sir," he said smiling.

What a pillock!

'Come out,' said the teacher who had asked the question while reaching into the cupboard for Black Sam. Black Sam was a short, thick cane that was wrapped in black tape. George walked to the front of the class, head bowed, and waited.

'Bend down'.

Thwack!

Goodbye school.

'Don't become an engineer, or you will always be an engineer,' said my Dad trying to guide me in my career. 'Work in an office where there are promotion prospects'. What's promotion I thought, but I followed his wishes. I delivered the mail. You always start off as the post boy then you work your way up I was told when I first arrived. I got bored quickly. The only good side to the job was that I met the girls who worked in the office, but that wasn't enough to keep me there. I went into engineering. Milling, turning, fitting and grinding were the order of the day and I loved it.

We worked opposite each other across wide benches in the fitting shop and quite often our toecaps would be tucked below it, I'd take this opportunity to crawl under the bench and paint toe-caps white. Another one of my impish things was to tie a piece of string to a nut on the back of a chuck on a lathe. I would lower the string down the back of the lathe, attach a plastic cup to the other end of the string and fill it with water. The consequence being that when the lathe operator turned on the machine, the chuck would spin forwards. The string would wind itself around the chuck and the plastic cup of water would be propelled upwards throwing its contents over the operator. I was suspended for three days once when I filled a large tank of coolant with soap powder. Two powerful pumps pumped the coolant onto the job to keep it cool and the ensuing soap suds-filled half the factory. We wore brown three-quarter length light brown jackets which had large open pockets on the side. The pockets were a total invite for anything and my cigarette butts finished up in a lot of these pockets. It took a while for the material of the jacket to start smoldering and you would see the person wearing the jacket start looking around and sniffing. Eventually he would twig, look down and begin beating his pocket. My apprenticeship finished when I was twenty-one and I emerged as a universal grinder.

There were parties, as there always is in your teens. At one party, one of the lads was holding a bottle of wine, while I was holding an empty glass. I proffered the glass to him and he ran out of the house shouting,

'Catch me and I'll fill your glass!'

The chase was on. He exited the house, ran up the road and across a patch of lawn that was surround by low hawthorn bushes. He jumped over the hawthorn bushes and I followed, but I didn't quite make it. My right foot just grazed the top of the hawthorn bushes. It was enough to unbalance me and down I went with the hand holding the glass beneath me, it was back to the hospital for more stitches. The nurse said that there was no doctor available right now to administer a pain killing injection and would I mind if she just carried on and stitched. I ouched eight times.

My girlfriend became pregnant and in those days you did the honorable thing, as we perceived it then. We lived with my Mum and Dad initially and that's where our eldest daughter was born. We bought our own house and two years later our son was born.

That's it I told myself, no more children. But, life's not that simple. Fourteen years later, along came Jane.

I was becoming bored again and wanted to move on. My brother-in-law worked for the GPO (now BT) as it was then known. He explained what he did and I found it rather exciting, so I went for an interview and soon began installing telephones. Three years later I was talking to a cousin who had his own taxi, worked from home and was his own boss, the lure was there. To raise capital for the taxi business meant selling the house and moving in with my Mum again. Dad wasn't there anymore.

I worked my nuts off to keep the two-car taxi business afloat but I was not a business man. Someone told the council that a business was operating from a council house without permission, and I was told that I had to leave as my Mum had not applied for us to live there, or run a business from there. I had a wife and two children to support and I was out on the streets. Where do I go from here?

The answer came from one of my brothers-in-law. He lived in a two up two down with his wife and three children. There were now four adults and five children living in his two up two down and it wasn't easy. Worst of all the cars were breaking down and business was not exactly booming. The business folded and I signed on for the first time in my life. I was only on the dole for one week when I got a job as a lorry driver. Lorry driving was followed by selling investment trusts for Bernie Cornfeld who siphoned off millions of pounds and the company nearly folded. My brother-in-law had been in the Royal Signals, but because of a knee injury he was given a medical discharge. He told me all about the army, and once again in life I became fired up at the new prospect. It would be the start of an exciting new career and, the army provided accommodation. I was lucky as the army had had a bad recruiting year and they had raised the intake age limit. I was twenty-six years old and got in by the skin of my teeth. Trade training followed basic training and I became a Linesman who dealt with the provision and maintenance of telephone lines. My previous experience with the GPO helped and I was asked if I would like to stay on at 8th Signal Regiment, and assist in the wiring of the new training school that was being built. Catterick was one of the few places where there were a reasonable number of married-quarters so my family soon joined me.

The army was just what I expected, different, and exciting. Tug 'O' War was the sport I first became interested in. It was the most energy sapping sport I have ever done. We would pull our guts out at one end of the rope. Then we would stand up and walk to the other end of the rope with knees that wouldn't support us and bodies that would not stop shaking, then we would do it all again, and possibly again as it was the best of three pulls. My first operation was due to my love of tug 'O' war. I bust a cartilage on one pull and went into hospital to have the cartilage removed. In those days the scalpel removed the damaged cartilage and you remained in hospital for three weeks. Today they just drill into your knee and pull the cartilage out, and you walk away. Another cartilage, a vasectomy and two wisdom teeth removal operations waited for me later in life, plus the odd extra stitches. I also popped my shoulder bone out of its socket, but I won't tell you about that right now as it appears in more detail later in the book.

There was time to do adventure training, then. Rock climbing in Norway, skiing in Austria with two long lengths of plastic clipped to my feet. Jumping out of a plane in Germany with a parachute attached to my back. Canoeing, orienteering, squash and badminton, the more sedate sports, the older I got. We had time to do sport, then! Today the army is so over committed and under manned that there is no time for fun.

Catterick – Germany – Edinburgh – Germany – Catterick again UGH! – Gibraltar – Blandford Forum with world travel, and that's where my story begins. Belize. Northern Ireland, and that's where my story ends. After Northern Ireland I was posted to Germany for two years then the UK for discharge. There were good times and bad times, but I don't regret doing the twenty two years.

ACKNOWLEDGEMENTS

He had his head poked into an electrical distribution panel when I walked into the factory, all I could see were his blue overalls dressing his slim body and his pony-tail hanging down between his shoulder blades. He turned around, peered over his glasses and said.

'Good morning'.

Each time I entered the factory we seemed to finish up talking together and the more we talked the more he surprised me. John, I discovered, was writing a thesis on some obscure Roman general for his Masters and he spoke Greek fluently.

'I'm doing a bit of writing,' I told him one day and explained the story line.

'Would you like me to check it over for you?' he asked.

John read every chapter, dotted my i's and crossed my t's and became known as my red ink man. John, what can I say but a huge thank you.

The biggest thank you goes to my loving wife Sue who put up with many lonely nights while I wrote this book. She gave me lots of space and never once complained.

Thanks Sue.

1

COMMUNICATIONS PROJECT DIVISION

You'll love it at Communications Project Division everyone told me as I would be flying to military bases around the world installing telecommunications systems. But, for the first six months of my posting, I had idled my time away waiting for it to happen. The problem was that the cable installation in Belize had been deferred. The Hong Kong project had been cancelled as we would soon be handing Hong Kong back to China and the radio network on the Rock of Gibraltar had been delayed indefinitely. True, the one on Ascension was still on, but that was seven months away! What really hacked me off was that the riggers were on the go all the time, buzzing around the UK and working in civvies (So no one would know it was a military installation) and staying in hotels.

There was definitely a shortage of riggers.

THOUGHT!!!!!! (But I wasn't too clever at heights)

THOUGHT!!!!! (Do I want to fester in this place?)

I visited the course booking clerk and got the number of the RAF Rigging School at Digby and my luck was in, a course was starting on Monday and there was one place left. "Sir," I said to Colonel Pat Soward, "There's a place on a rigging course that starts next Monday, it's a six week course and I've got nothing on until the Ascension job."

At forty-three I was the oldest student on the course and the one with the least hair. "It's been years since we had someone your age," said the veteran flight sergeant rigger who had the 'I've seen it, done it, been there' map etched on his face, and the 'throw what you like at me world, I'll cope with it' look in his eyes. One of his calloused hands pointed upwards, "The climbing test's first," he said, then he paused for effect, and slammed the next sentence into us "If you fail that you're on the next train out."

The climbing test was on a 365-feet tower that sat on top of a hill forty-five minutes drive away, and the merest mention of that tower thrust fear into those who had failed, and triumph into those that had succeeded. I looked around the coach, and no matter whose eyes I looked into I could see fear lurking, except, that is, for the veteran flight sergeant, he was tried and tested. He probably sat in the same position on every journey at the back of the bus, slouching against a window, with his left arm draped across the back of the seat, legs crossed, with a slightly bemused and nonchalant look on his face as he picked out the ones that he felt wouldn't make it. He'd heard all the nervous gags being bantered around from previous hopefuls, our names were different, but the looks on our faces were the same.

We gathered at the base of the tower with butterflies of fear fluttering around our stomachs, and waited for the flight sergeant,

"The rules are simple," he began.

"FIRST – you go up the central ladder to the one-hundred-feet stage where you will have a rope attached to you. You will then climb out onto the outside of a leg and make your way down to the ground.

SECOND – You will climb up to the two-hundred-feet stage where once again you will have a rope attached. Then you will climb out onto the outside of a leg, and make your way down to the one-hundred-feet stage.

THIRD – You will climb up to the top of the tower where I will be waiting to make sure you do it, and then you will make your way down to the ground."

There was going to be no time wasted on this dull, windy and overcast Autumn day, as soon as the Flight Sergeant had finished his sermon one of the two Corporals flanking him immediately stabbed a finger forward twice, "YOU and YOU," he yelled. The two volunteers' shoulders sagged, then they lifted their heads, took a deep breath, and stepped forward, the rest of us craned our necks and watched as they climbed, sat astride an eight inch wide girder at one hundred-feet, edged their way out to the outside leg and slithered down to the ground. No one failed step one and a feeling of bravado rippled through us as we laughed and joked on the climb up towards step two at the two-hundred-feet stage where we huddled in silence, buried our heads in our jackets to protect them from the strong chill easterly wind. We bent our knees in unison as the tower swayed, and felt that they had seriously underestimated the height.

"YOU!" yelled the Corporal stabbing his finger again. Everyone sensed a forward motion in me but there was no movement, I felt that my feet were super glued to the platform, and I didn't want to produce a solvent. The Corporals smiled as the flight sergeant broke the bond with a push in my back and even then I seemed to linger before jerking forward two steps.

The steel work got thinner the higher you climbed, and I now found myself astride a three inch wide girder edging out towards an outside leg. Half way out several girders came together that formed a kind of web that I had to negotiate and the only way forward was to raise my legs over them. I paused, gulped down the fear that was rising, took a deep breath, raised my left leg to loop it over a girder and that forced me to lean to my right and look down. The ground seemed to be hundreds of miles below and the fear that had been gently fluttering in my stomach suddenly buzzed wildly, and after my second attempt to raise my leg over a girder I decided it couldn't be done without falling sideways.

Incoming verbal from the instructors rang momentarily in my ears before being snatched away by the strong breeze, "Get a move on!" they shouted. I completely shut down. It was now just me, and the girder. Nothing else mattered. I took deep breaths and closed my mind to everything except that girder. I'd made a decision, instead of raising my leg slowly, I'd flick it over quickly so that it would just drop over the other side, but I wasn't ready for the big sideways heave it gave me, which took my mind off what I was doing and left me with my heel resting on the girder. I was now tilted at an angle of forty degrees with my heel stuck on THAT girder, my heart pounded, my ears rushed, panic was just a couple of microns away waiting to dive in and put me on the next train home. I took a deep breath, AGAIN, concentrated, edged forwards slightly and that caused me to tilt even more. Maybe it was the fear, or maybe my leg just twitched without me knowing it but my leg miraculously slipped over, and thankfully my body righted itself.

DON'T STOP NOW, I told myself.

I left my fingerprints embedded in the steel of that girder but with four more girders to cross I'd learnt my lesson. I inched myself forwards to the next girder, paused, took a deep breath, gripped the girder that I was sitting on and swung my leg up and over, it was a piece of cake.

The outside legs of the tower were triangular in shape with the 'V' of the girder pointing outwards, and the drill was to grip the edges of the girder with your hands and dig the instep of your wellies (Wellies were better for braking they had told us) into the edges of the girder at the same time. Left hand down twelve inches, left foot down twelve inches, grip with left hand and dig instep of left foot into the leg of mast, then right hand down twelve inches and right foot down twelve inches, grip with right hand and dig inset of right foot into the leg of the mast. Slowly but surely I was making my way down the one hundred feet to the next platform, but half way there my arms began to tire and I realised that I no longer had the strength to grip tightly, my descent began to speed up and that panic feeling made itself known to me again, I was clueless as to how to get out of this one. It was the verbal from the instructors that saved me, "Bend your knees!" they shouted, and I did. I was now calmly resting at one hundred and fifty feet with my knees bent, wellies dug in, looking around admiring the view and in total control of the situation. The verbal from the instructors changed, "Get a move on," they now shouted, I felt good.

I climbed back up to the two-hundred-feet stage and whilst regaining my breath I watched the next would be rigger who had exactly the same problem as I did. When he reached the web of girders, he also felt that he would fall over when he raised his leg, and the shouts and threats from the instructors streamed towards him until he moved on. His ascent down the outside leg began slowly, but speeded up as he reached the one hundred and fifty feet point as his arms began to tire and he went into panic mode, he couldn't take on board the shouts from the instructors and his high-pitched scream echoed down the valleys as his hands began to burn and he let go. He swung slowly, face down on the end of his safety line, with his arms outstretched trying to grab steel, and when he did he clung on to it like a baby monkey hanging onto its mother. Great heaves of 'Thank God I'm alright' racked his body, then when he had calmed, and got his mind back together he completed the climb.

The next would be rigger was severely rattled and he only got as far as the web of girders before he froze solid and took on the thousand yard stare. The instructors changed tactics and instead of yelling they used friendly coercion whilst tugging gently on the rope, but it was no use, he'd gone. "Haul him in," said the exasperated Flight Sergeant but the two Corporals did not have the combined strength to break his vice like grip so the Flight Sergeant assisted and stamped on his fingers, then he popped up like a sunken cork surfacing and gently rotated. His eyes were vacant, the size of saucers, and his face was Dulux brilliant white. "We don't have time to take him down, tie him to the rail and we'll sort him out later," said the Flight Sergeant. Sympathy abounded!!

There was only one thing left for me to do, climb the remaining one hundred and sixty five feet to the top of the tower but I made the mistake of following just a few rungs below the Flight Sergeant's lumbering lope, and he purposefully bounced and whistled as though out on a Sunday walk as he climbed the thirty-feet long wooden ladders that gave access to the next platform. The higher we climbed the more my nerves jangled and the situation became too much, I had to stop and put some distance between the two of us. At three-hundred-feet the wind was howling and I had never realised that steel could so flexible and bend so much without breaking. The tower swayed like a yacht being tossed around in a gale force nine and I had to stop several more times to gulp down the fear that constantly rose inside me. With just sixty-five feet to go there was no way I was backing out so with slightly shaking hands and knocking knees I made it to the top platform where he stood totally relaxed, leaning gently on a rail, smoking a fag and admiring the view. He turned, smiled, and gave me the thumbs up as though this was an everyday experience while I felt that I had just conquered Everest. On the way down I passed the rigger who had bottled out, and he was still roped to the platform rail.

Back in the classroom we were one man short, and what followed was six pleasant weeks of antenna theory, antenna propagation, learning the different types of cables and working on forty-foot masts. To keep us out of mischief in the evenings the staff had organised a sports competition that everyone had to participate in. Squash, badminton and table tennis were knockout competitions that we organised ourselves whilst the running, shot putting, hop skip and jump, long jump and high jump were monitored by the instructors. It was all good, clean, energetic and competitive fun and being the older one I was better at the racket sports and long-distance running. I was top of the leader board right up to the end then a six-feet-one inch thirteen-stone Welshman won the shot put and scooped ten points.

I returned to my Unit on a Friday and rolled into the office, "How did you get on?" asked Colonel Soward. "Sir, I passed," I said feeling all cocky and sure of myself. "Good, you fly out to Canada on Tuesday and take Ian with you," he said. Ian was our driver who constantly complained that all he did was to take people to airports but never went anywhere himself. I walked out shaking my head, chuckling and disbelieving what I had just heard, and made my way to the workshops. An hour later a civvie project manager came and briefed me.

CANADA

The Rocky Mountains towered above Calgary on this warm autumn day and the sun glinting off their snow-capped peaks made me squint as I admired them from the top of the aircraft steps. The view entranced me and filled me with a feeling of awe and it wasn't until a stewardess said, "Move on please," that I realised that I was partially blocking the stairway. I, like many other arrivals would be warned that the temperature could change from plus twenty to minus-twenty degrees Centigrade in one hour if the wind direction changed and swept towards us from The Rockies.

Our three-hour bus journey to BATUS (British Army Training Unit Suffield) took us across rolling hills which were followed by more rolling hills that were three thousand feet above sea level and went on for three thousand miles. I found the vast emptiness of The Prairies interesting to begin with but after half an hour it became boring as the hill in front looked exactly like the one behind. The lack of pollution at this height allowed me to see far into the distance where a water tower or a 'donkey' nodding up and down pumping oil or gas up from the bowels of the earth looked very close but took an eon to reach. I could see why the British Army had chosen Suffield for a live firing range.

I bumped into the mover (Personnel movement administrator) in the mess that night and he asked how long I would be staying. I explained that I had no idea as my briefing wasn't until the following morning, but asked if this would create a problem. "Well, there's one flight every three weeks to the UK, and if you just miss one you will have to take a civilian flight to Washington DC, stay overnight and catch the Belize flight." It got me thinking!

The following morning Ian and I waited in a corridor in HQ for Captain Ferguson to arrive and as we waited an officer holding a piece of paper crossed the corridor and entered another office so we saluted and said Good Morning. Thirty seconds later another officer came out of his office, crossed the corridor holding his piece of paper so once again we saluted and said Good Morning. A couple of minutes later another officer crossed the corridor holding a piece of paper, which caused an image to appear in my mind of clockwork toys programmed to pick up a piece of paper when they heard voices outside, walk across the corridor, get a salute, and then return to their office with a smug smile on their faces. "Berets off," I told Ian, "I can't stand this crap anymore."

"Good morning," said a chirpy six-footer with glasses. "Captain Ferguson?" I enquired! "Yes," he said extending his right hand and then beckoning us into his office. "I want the two existing antennae on *Brutus* (a long slim mast located in the middle of the firing range that would be as easy to climb as a two hundred-feet ladder!!), raising to provide better coverage. I also want two new antennae rigged, one on top of the mast and the other one just below it." He outlined a few other tasks then asked, "How long do you think it will take?" "About four weeks," I replied.

Ian and I picked up a Land Rover, loaded our gear, and then drove along the dusty clay rippled Rattlesnake Road to *Brutus* where we surveyed the scene. Three of the tasks were pretty straightforward, but I couldn't work out how to rig the antennae on to the top of the mast as it consisted of a twelve-foot long aluminium pole that had four small antennae attached. I imagined myself lifting the twelve-foot long pole and trying to slot it down the neck of the mast, and then holding it with one hand whilst bolting it up with the other. It was an impossible task for two riggers, never mind one. What I needed was a gin pole that could be attached to the side of the mast, but where do you find one of those in the middle of The Prairies?

The fear of heights still lurked within me so to build up my confidence I began working at the lowest level possible, one hundred and forty feet. My ascent was easy to begin with but became harder and harder, and my rest stops were more frequent the higher I climbed. I couldn't work why it was becoming so difficult until I looked down, then I realised that the rope that was attached to my belt was getting longer and heavier. My shakes became shakier as I neared my goal, and another rest with lots of deep breaths was needed.

I reached my goal, clung onto the mast with one hand, wrapped my belt around a strut with the other, then clipped on my belt, and with slightly trembling fingers got on with the task. Two hours later I was back on the ground and when I had finished my coffee I looked up, and realised my bottle had gone as my mind kept repeating 'NO! NO! NO! "We'll knock off early and go and see Captain Ferguson about the top antenna," I explained to Ian, in the hope that my face didn't show what I was feeling.

I explained the problem to Captain Ferguson then gulped when he said, "No problem. I'll book a chopper for us. Two days should give you enough time to get everything sorted." I had a few beers in the mess that night to calm my nerves, but they didn't work, so I had a few more.

The stiff morning breeze blew my hangover away the following day as I climbed two hundred feet to the top of *Brutus* and once there I did a quick survey to see how and what would be required. The lowering of the antenna was not a problem, but the chopper would have to hover and wait until the aluminium pole had been bolted on. I decided a wooden base plate would need to be manufactured which would be inserted across the struts of the mast so that the pole could then rest on it and the chopper wouldn't have to hover, but what size would the base plate need to be? Cursing I descended, grabbed a tape rule, climbed to the top again and measured the distance between the struts. Back on terra firma I was knackered, totally knackered and that all too familiar knock of my knees told me that it was time to call it a day. "We're going back to camp to get a base-plate made," I told Ian.

It was a simple item for the Canadian carpenter to produce and he handed it over to me with a nonchalant smile and the words, "Glad to be at your service Brit." It was only one o'clock, but I decided that I couldn't face *Brutus* again that day. "There's no point in going back this afternoon," I told Ian, "We'll knock off early."

My second day's hangover was blown away the same way as the first day's hangover, and I spent six hours rigging on that bastard *Brutus* and although my hands still trembled slightly, I realised that my confidence was improving.

On the third day we met Captain Ferguson at nine, and he informed us that everything was still on schedule and that the chopper would be arriving at half-ten. Ian and I had prepared everything the day before, and the aluminium pole with the four antennae attached lay on the ground, waiting to be hoisted. Captain Ferguson and I fastened on our climbing belts, and then we both gazed into the distance and waited for the chopper to arrive. There was nothing to see except rolling hills rolling onto more rolling hills then a silent black speck appeared in the distance which got bigger and bigger. The beat of its blades began to tickle our ears, grow louder until it overwhelmed us as it hovered overhead and slipped gently to the ground. Ian and I humped the aluminium pole that had a thirty-feet length of rope tied near to its top over to the chopper where the loadmaster attached a quick release hook and tested our two-way radios. Captain Ferguson went first and he climbed effortlessly, (I later discovered that he was an avid rock climber, so I wasn't too pissed off) while I struggled to keep up with him, and when I finally reached the top he radioed the chopper.

The choppers downdraught had the ferocity of a hurricane in the tropics and the heavy beat of its blades bludgeoned its way into the depths of my ears. I squinted through my eyes and watched the chopper that was hovering thirty-seven feet above us with the pole swinging gently below, but it was slightly off target and too high, but closing in. As the pole drifted towards me I reached out, just managed to catch it with the tips of my fingers and tried to drag it towards me, but the chopper drifted off and dragged me with it. I was at full stretch looking up. The clouds above me seemed to accelerate across the sky and the noise, the down draught, the vertigo and my aching arm made me slightly dizzy and I thought I was on my way down.

I let go of the pole and my thoughts calmed a little as I realised that I was still at the top of the mast and in one piece. The chopper was coming in again, creeping towards us ever so slowly, but this time I didn't reach for the pole until it was directly above us. The chopper's roar seemed to create an envelope of noise around us that cut out the rest of the world and an eerie feeling crept into me as I looked up at the pole drifting downwards against a background of blurring blades, with the loadmaster staring down through goggled eyes. It was easy this time, the pilot was spot on so I grabbed the pole and guided it into the neck of the mast and waved my arm in a downward manner until the bottom of the pole rested on the base plate. Captain Ferguson spoke into his radio, "Release." The rope snaked down, wrapped itself around the pole, then the chopper soared upwards, banked sharply and buzzed off into the distance like a giant bumble bee heading home leaving us with a gentle breeze, peace and serenity. It was over, another experience under my belt, and it all seemed so easy, now. "I'll leave you to it now the fun's over," said Ferguson smiling and unclipping his belt.

After clamping the pole to the inside of the mast I looked up and sighed as I realised it wasn't over yet, the rope would need to be removed. Stepping onto the top of the mast I wrapped my belt around the pole and I wasn't at all happy with my situation as I realised I would have to climb even higher to reach the knot. Alarm bells clanged big style in my head as I climbed onto the lowest antennae and the pole leaned slightly, 'There's no way this pole is going to snap' I told myself, so once again I waited until my fear was 'under control' and just when I stepped up onto the next antenna one of those freak gusts of wind that comes out of the middle of nowhere chose that moment to arrive.

The pole leaned to what I felt was ninety degrees and I clung on to it and shit myself. So, there I was, clinging to a pole on top of a two-hundred-feet mast in the middle of The Prairies with soiled underpants, and once again wondering how the hell I'd got myself into this situation. I made my way down, slowly, and as I neared the ground Ian shouted up, "What about the rope?" I clenched my buttocks hoping that he couldn't see the stain and said, "It'll have to stay. I can't reach it!" If you ever go to the British Army's live firing range in Suffield, Canada, look at the top of a mast called *Brutus,* the rope is probably still there!

It was Ian's turn to do the hard work the following day and I watched as he hauled on a rope that was attached to the feeder cable, it rose slowly and when it arrived I connected it to the antenna, waterproof taped the joint, and then made my way down, stopping every six rungs to zip tie the cable to the mast. My confidence should have been improving but, when I was half way down, I lost my bottle, (again) so I hung onto the mast, rested and thought, 'Do I really have to do this'? I got truly wrecked that night.

Next day, I stood with one foot on the first rung of the mast and looked up at *Brutus* the Bastard, and it took a huge mental effort to begin climbing again. At one hundred and fifty feet my hangover began to fade and I congratulated myself with a smile as I realised that I was beginning to enjoy the climb and the fear that had constantly lurched in my stomach had faded.

Medicine Hat had been so named because an Indian medicine man had lost his hat just before the tribe had been defeated in battle. It was the closest town to Suffield and Ian and I decided to spend a weekend there, so we booked a double room in the Sinoboia Hotel, or, as it has it had been aptly named, 'The Sin Bin'. Your feet stuck to the carpet, the furniture was basic, waiter service was great, the beer was great, it had a fast talking DJ, drop dead gorgeous strippers and a rowdy smokey atmosphere. What more could a squaddie ask for? With a twinkle in our eyes and an impish smile on our faces we poured from the jug, chinked our glasses, grinned at each other across the table and got stuck into the night.

Rush hour in the bathroom was just after a stripper had performed, and when I entered all the urinals were occupied, so I ducked into a toilet and openly laughed when I saw the grey porcelain top of the water closet chained to the bottom part. I zipped up, and still chuckling, turned and walked straight into a six-feet two inches tall four feet wide mobile brick wall who had tribal scars and a 'look at you little man' grin on its face. I was VERY, VERY deferential to the Red Indian.

Hoots, whistles and yahoos rose from the crowd, drinkers stood on stools and tables to get the best possible view and the night moved on up when the next stripper came on stage. I spoke to one group of soldiers who told me they had booked a flight to the States for eight days of their ten days R&R but after two nights in The Sin Bin they had cancelled their flight, lost their deposit and decided to stay there for the next eight days. It was a wild and woolly red neck weekend that I'll never forget.

Our work was coming to an end as *Brutus* had been rigged, the radio room cables had been rerouted, and the maintenance on the existing antennae had been carried out but one task remained. The military staff at Calgary airport had no means of communicating with incoming or outgoing flights and our task was to rig an antenna on the roof of Calgary Airport and run its feeder cable down seven floors to their office in the basement. I told Captain Ferguson that the antennae would take three days to install, but after an early completion we still had one and a half days to enjoy ourselves in a good hotel with a generous meal allowance in our pockets.

The first bar we entered in Calgary just happened to be a strip bar and on the table next to us were two cowboys with Stetson hats, bootlace ties and cowboy boots, "Are you English?" asked one of them. They were totally friendly, as most Canadians are and they offered to take us on a tour of the bars. Four bars later we were watching a stripper who was introduced as the next centrefold spread of Penthouse, and she was drop dead gorgeous. She danced semi naked to her first record, stripped off to her second record, and then danced totally naked to the third and she was the best contortionist I have ever seen.

If you wanted to show your appreciation you could roll up a dollar bill, hold it between your teeth then lay on the edge of the stage and wait for her to extract it with her tits. I went through twenty dollars that night. An announcement came over the mike, "Will the two British soldiers please stand up." The two cowboys looked at Ian and myself and raised their hands palms up, so we rose and to our surprise we got a round of applause and people we had never met before bought us beers and shook our hands. It was another great night.

Ian had been dying, busting and gagging for a pee all the way back in the cab and when we staggered out of the lift on the fourth floor he couldn't wait to walk down the long corridor to his room. The chunks of ice falling into the tray of the coke machine opposite the lift were just too much for him to bear and with a look of relief on his face he held his head back as steam rose upwards. BEWARE of yellow ice!

Next day we ate an in-flight breakfast and drank champagne courtesy of Canadian Airlines, then changed at Salt Lake City and flew on to Washington D.C. To save our travelling expenses for other pleasures, we checked the equivalent of Yellow Pages and searched for the cheapest accommodation possible. Economy Hotels listed a hotel on 'I' street, and when we arrived we asked the cab to wait, just in case. We rang the bell on the locked bullet proof door then waited until a security guard slid back a small shutter and peered out at us through metal bars. The guard gave us the once over, closed the shutter, slid back steel bars and creaked open the door. After booking in we found our way to our room that was acceptable, just, and if you wanted to hide your money the safest place was under the soap.

We were hungry and ready for a few beers after our journey so we quickly showered, changed and headed into town but there was a problem, it was Thanks Giving Day and most of Washington was closed! We eventually spotted a flickering neon sign down a side street that beckoned us like a curled finger and when we entered the bar a blast of warm air, soul music and a bunch of lively local people welcomed us in. After ordering beers the usual question was asked, followed by the usual statement, 'I love your accent'! The bar was a replica of Cheers and we had one brilliant night. We both wished that the evening could have gone on for longer but after the previous night out and the travelling the yawns set in. We began to say goodbye to everyone then Brad, who was dressed in a chauffeurs' uniform asked us where we were staying. What a guy! Outside he bowed slightly as he opened the rear door of a black stretch limousine and proffered his hand. We couldn't believe our luck as we sank into luxurious seats and stretched out our legs, then Brad's voice came over the intercom, "Help yourselves to a drink," whereupon slow easy jazz drizzled in.

Outside our hotel, Brad said that he would wait until we were safely inside as this was not the nicest part of town, and I'll always remember the look of dismay on the security guard's face as he slid back the shutter and saw the stretch limo. I lay awake listening to Ian crunching crisps and after eating half of them he dropped the remainder on the floor and switched off the light. Room service visited our room during the night and when we awoke mice had cleared up his debris.

FALKLAND ISLAND

Trees that resembled old men leaning on walking sticks occasionally broke the boredom of the skyline, and signs stating 'MINEFIELD – DO NOT CROSS' stood proudly in front of lines of barbed wire.

Initially, Roomey (Lance Corporal Neild Roome) and I lived with the contractors as the military accommodation was still being built, and on our first night we wandered around to see what was on offer. The blue movie room was packed, as it was every night, except Thursday, when a quiz in their bar was livened up with questions such as, "Who said I hope all your doughnuts turn out like Fanny's?" answer – Johnny Craddock on their TV cook show.

Roomey and I were down there to build towers and rig antennae for a new communications network. Three metre dishes were required on most of the towers and after rigging our first dish Roomey and I gazed up with a smile on our faces, and slapped each other on the back. Then a technician wiped away our smiles, "It's upside down," he said. "Can't be," I told him with a smug expression, "I checked the orientation." We ignored him, he was a technician who worked in a warm environment and never got his hands cold or dirty, but he was insistent, "The drain hole in the plastic cover is at the top, so when it rains the dish will fill up with water and become too heavy!" he stated. I was dumbstruck. How did this pale faced, technical, in-door, centrally heated technician know this? But he was right. Roomey and I had had a tough day and now we had been usurped by, of all things, a TECHNICIAN!!! It was late afternoon and the euphoria that we had felt had gone, so I decided to leave the dish until the next day. It rained heavily that night!

The following morning we pondered our options. We could lower the three metre dish down to the ground, turn the plastic cover round so that the drain hole was at the bottom, and then raise it again, or we could drill a hole into the bottom of the plastic cover. I wrapped my belt around a strut just below the dish, leaned out until I was horizontal and, with my insteps pressing into a girder grabbed the brace and bit in my belt. With my arms at full stretch I tried to drill the hole but it was no use, I couldn't quite reach. On the ground I was shaking from the exertion and as we pondered our options a mobile crane came down the dusty track craning its neck and nodding like a giraffe drinking water as the driver increased his speed until the rear wheels rose off the ground, and then decelerated until they touched down again. I leapt out in front of the crane, waved my arms and asked the driver if he had half an hour to spare. "What's your problem?" he asked. "I need to drill a hole in the bottom of a plastic cover on that dish," I said pointing, "But I can't reach it. If I could sit on the end of your jib, could you raise me up?" After slithering up the grease splattered jib I sat on its tip and gave the thumbs up. The crane's engine roared and the chain that telescoped the jibs extensions clanked behind me. I was concerned about my heavily greased stained backside as one backward slip would have put my nuts onto the revolving chain and chewed them into mincemeat, which made me focus and concentrate with total commitment. By the time I got to the dish my arms were aching, my veins were throbbing and my arse was twitching. I gave the driver the thumbs up again and a great sigh of relief rippled through me when I heard the engine die to a quiet hum. I wasn't sure how long it would take for the jib to stop rising after my signal, and I realised that I had given the signal too early, so I pointed my finger into the air, grabbed hold of the jib and waited. But instead of hearing the engine roar, the jib silently dropped a few feet and my heart leapt into my mouth. I didn't even know the crane drivers name, but a few choice ones came to mind, I was confused as I thought that he had misunderstood. But he was very competent and he could see that if he continued to extend the jib at the same angle I would have finished up above where I needed to drill the hole. The engine revs increased as the jib extended then it fell to a low chugging murmur when my head was just below the bottom of the dish. I leaned slightly to my left to compensate for the wind as I withdrew the drill, and gripping the jib with my legs, I reached up and began to drill the hole. The thin plastic cover took seconds to drill through, but another problem arose. The overnight rain had collected inside the plastic cover and it now came out in a steady stream onto my head, and a roar of laughter rose from the onlookers below, even the crane driver was pointing up and laughing.

On the way home Roomey asked me to look after his camera as he had arranged a game of squash, and didn't want to leave it in the changing rooms. BIG MISTAKE. Back in my room I dropped my trousers, stood in front of the mirror and snapped away. When we got back to the UK, Roomey posted the film off for processing, and when they came back his wife opened them. She accused him of having a gay affair, and I had to go round to his house and explain the whole situation to her, but I don't think she believed me!!

ASCENSION ISLAND

Huge radio dishes that milked information from orbiting satellites squatted on the tops of flattened peaks of extinct volcanoes. Orange ash that had vomited from those volcanoes millions of years ago carpeted the whole of the island, and aircraft going south stopped here to refuel, as Ascension was roughly half way between the UK and The Falklands. Lava flows abounded, and I was informed that this was where the first lunar landing vehicle had been tested. The only green spot on Ascension was on the top of Green Mountain. In days gone by, when India had been our 'jewel in the crown', passing ships had called in for fresh water, and the only way they could pay for the water was with soil. It would have taken a couple of days for the sailors to hike up to the top of Green Mountain and back, therefore, donkeys were shipped in to carry the burden, and later released when the internal combustion engine was introduced. The sacks of soil grew until they became a meadow, and an evening stroll to the top of Green Mountain was an experience. You began your hot sweaty trek on orange volcanic ash, and ended it in the English countryside, where cows grazed, pigs grunted, and The Red Lion waited to quench your thirst with a cool pint of John Smiths, or Lager. The Guinness Book of Records (I was told) listed the golf course on Ascension as the worst golf course in the world, as its roughs were lava flows, and its greens were rolled orange volcanic ash.

Seven telecommunications engineers and I were on Ascension for eight weeks to install a cable network, a new telephone exchange and ancillary equipment. The work was interesting and the weather marvelous, and at the end of each day we quenched our parched throats in the bar. A variety show, who's next gig was five thousand miles due south, which consisted of a compere/comedian, rock band and four lady dancers came to entertain us one weekend. The comedian was uproarious, the band lifted our spirits and the dancers tantalised us. After the show we invited them back to the mess.

A rousing cheer erupted when three of the dancers arrived waving a pair of panties over their heads, then silence shunted in as the fourth one strolled to the centre of the mess, and looked coyly around. Those who couldn't see quickly shuffled forward and when she had everyone's utmost attention she smiled naughtily, slowly turned, looked into our eyes then stooped, slipped her hands up inside her skirt, tilted her face upwards, and with a glint in her eyes paused. My ears rushed and everybody's blink rate fell to zero as she slowly wriggled her bum and, very, very slowly, drew down her panties. Then she stepped out of one leg and, with a deft flick, sent them sailing towards the goggle eyed barman who caught them perfectly. We were charged up and semi erect as the barman sniffed them and gave the thumbs up, then he hung them behind the bar with previous donations. Female company in this male dominated environment was always an absolute pleasure, and just to talk to them made your day.

Lashings of good food and free flowing beer gave us a wonderfully satisfying glow in our stomachs, and we couldn't have asked for more, then someone in a kilt wailed in with his bagpipes. He began with 'Flower of Scotland', and continued with more songs that we could sing along to, and as he marched around the mess one person tagged on behind him, then another and another until the whole of the mess was tailing him in a long weaving conga. The Piper left the bar, entered the quadrangle, stepped down into the fishpond, stepped out the other side, and walked back into the mess, and everyone single one of us was wet from the knees down.

The talking got louder and the laughter became more drunkenly raucous as gaiety became the order of the night. The girls had probably been chatted up more in one night than they had in the past twelve months, and they had loved it, and so had we. They decided to leave us when they couldn't understand our slurring speech and we began to fall over. After the girls had left a RAF sergeant knelt down at a bar stool where the fourth dancer had been sitting and sniffed it, a queue quickly formed.

The following day a car hit a donkey. It was the first fatal road accident that the policeman (there was no local population on Ascension, the workforce came from Saint Helena) had dealt with, so he read the rulebook and followed it to the letter. The chalk outline of the dead donkey remained on the road until the next rain fell. There was no duty on booze on Ascension.

Drink prices in the mess:

Brandy - 2p
Gin   - 2p
Vodka - 1 & ½p
Pint   - 40p
Coke   - 30p

Only doubles were served and every Friday a two for the price of one Happy Hour took place, but as vodka was 1 & 1/2p, and the barman didn't want to be bothered with half pence's, he served double doubles instead.

BELIZE

The gentle breeze that whispered around my body was just enough to keep the thirty-three degrees and ninety percent humidity bearable on my six month tour of Belize. Today was going to be a no hurry day, one that had to be savoured at a slow pace and when I arrived at the zoo I paused at a hitching rail type fence, smoked a lazy cigarette and gazed into a pond on the other side. Slow ripples wrinkled out from the centre of the pond as a fish broke the surface and fed off whatever was unlucky enough to have landed at the wrong place at the wrong time. I continued to watch the fish's mouth as it lingered, oddly, just above the surface, then a small black snout and two cold glassy eyes appeared. I found a zoo attendant, quickly, and told her. She smiled at me and in a calming voice said, "Its fine, he lives there." "But he can get out." "He does disappear for two or three days sometimes, but he always comes back," she said walking off with a cock of the head. I later learnt that the Belizean crocodile was a small variety that normally fed off small animals and fish, or, occasionally, tiny children, but it had never been known to attack an adult.

My day continued with my first trip to the city of Belize and when I looked around I thought, 'what City' (This was twenty years ago. There has been a lot of investment since then). The bank, the government offices, the hotels and the supermarkets were the only brick buildings. The rest were built of wood and every time a hurricane whistled through they rebuilt them. The pavements were major trade outlets that were lined with goods that started with A, and ended in Z, and I couldn't even put a name to some of them.

Chickens, that were clueless to the fate that lay ahead of them, sat quietly in a line with their feet tethered and their heads bobbing up and down and left and right. Freshly slaughtered black meat hung from hooks, and to inspect a cut you waved your hand and the meat would turn red as a swarm of black flies became airborne. Igies (iguanas) lay flat on their bellies and looked up at you through pained eyes, as to prevent them from running away their legs had been broken, pulled up over their backs and tied together. I walked down a side street but after venturing twenty yards, I did a quick U turn as the scenery went down market dramatically. Getting mugged in Belize City, then, was guaranteed if you were on your own. Standing orders forbade visiting the city after eighteen hundred hours alone, but if you were stupid enough to do so, the Military Police would pick you up and the penalty was fourteen days nick.

A free coach, courtesy of the Ministry of Defence was laid on each evening to take squaddies into Belize City, or to The Rose Garden (the local brothel), so one Saturday night, after tanking up on duty frees several of us jumped aboard. The coach was filled with members of a parachute battalion and five minutes into our journey I watched as two Paras slid open their windows, stood on their seats and climbed out on to the roof. I leaned out of my window, looked up at the thick chrome luggage rail that ran around the roof, and giggled in amazement. The two Paras were standing on the roof with their legs apart, knees bent slightly, one arm stretched out in front, the other stretched out behind and they leaned forward to compensate for the forty miles per hour breeze as they surfed to Belize City.

A car pulled up in front of us as walked down the main street and the driver climbed out, left his door open, the engine running and went over to talk to someone. The 'Imp' took control of me and without thinking I sat in the car and revved the engine. I imagined the driver rushing towards me thinking that his car was being stolen and I climbed out chuckling to myself. But I'll never do that again – the feel of a cold black steel gun barrel held to my head rattled me.

Three Belizean dollars (about sixty pence) was the entry fee to the 'Upstairs Café', and our store-man Jim, had come up with a cunning plan to get us in free. To allow you to leave and return without having to pay twice, the doormen ticked the back of your hand with a highlight pen. We waited in a pub nearby, and when Jim returned he said, "It's orange on the right hand," and pulled out a pack of coloured high light pens. Jim, grinning jubilantly marked the back of our outstretched hands and when he came to himself, he ticked the back of his hand several times just to be sure. Jim lingered at the back as we dodged holes on the stair carpet to the Upstairs Cafe, and he watched as the doorman shone a florescent light onto the back of our hands.

We could tell by the doorman's guarded whispers to his mate that they knew that they had not seen us arrive or leave that evening. But what could they do? Jim had a huge triumphal smile on his face when he saw we were being admitted, but his smile turned to one of despair when they checked his hand. There was a scramble of ticks on the back and they made him pay. It was not a good tour for Jim, two months later he leaned over the balcony at the Upstairs Café, slipped and splattered on the pavement below. He was casi-vac'd back to the UK with serious injuries.

One of the resident battalion's jobs was to patrol the border between Belize and Guatemala, and to enable them to communicate back to HQ a rebroadcast station was needed. The rebroadcast station (rebro) was a vehicle that sat on top of a hill in the depths of the jungle, and its job was to capture messages from the patrol, and then rebroadcast them.

The rebro needed re-supplying on a regular basis and the Yeoman of Signals, Nobby (Stiles), decided to accompany the driver on one of those runs. "I couldn't believe it," said Nobby in the mess that night, "There we were, completely lost, driving along a dirt road with a dust cloud billowing behind us, thick jungle on either side, clueless as to where we were, and we came across this grey haired seventy years old lady. She was sitting in the shade on a rocking chair with a shotgun on her lap next to a straw hut with a Coca-Cola sign hanging from it, and a generator humming that kept her fridge chilled. She told us that she had once been married to a British squaddie, but had fallen in love with Belize so much that when he left she had remained. Then there was a scurrying noise so she lifted up the shot-gun, fired into the roof of the hut and yelled, F--king Rats."

At the three-month point of our tour we could go back to the UK, or invite someone to holiday with us on the Keys or in Mexico. Chris, a long, gangly, six feet tall, white skinned, freckled, twenty three years old technician, told me what he was going to do for his two weeks R&R. He explained that being in Belize created a real problem for him when it came to watching his favourite soap, 'Home and Away'. To overcome this problem, he said he had asked his girlfriend to record every episode, so that when he flew home he would be able to catch up by watching four hours of tapes a day. But that created another problem for him, as he couldn't watch the episodes being televised or he would have gone out of sequence, so he said that he was going to tape them and slot them in at the end. Mind blowing stuff! My first impression of Chris completely changed when our paths crossed again. He proved that he had balls when we later worked together rigging antennae in Northern Ireland where we provided communications for SAS operations.

The funniest of all incidents that occurred on this tour happened one Saturday morning when I marched the troop down to the garages for a cleanup operation. Two large steel plates had been laid across a trench in the road and the gap between them had been packed with clay. The combination of ninety-percent humidity, occasional rain and lots of sunshine had baked the clay rock hard. People could walk across the clay, but the constant rhythmical slam of boots when soldiers are marching is a different thing.

The first four soldiers of the centre file were lucky, but not the fifth. When he stamped on the clay it crumbled and he slipped into the gap and hung there with one arm resting on each plate and his head and shoulders above.

The soldiers behind him didn't stand a chance and as the pile of bodies grew they created a stumbling block for the two outer files. It was so funny that I developed a giggling fit and practically wet myself as I watched the first twelve soldiers carry on marching down the road, while the pile of bodies behind them grew higher and higher. It was a scene straight out of 'Dad's Army', and I fell on the grass at the side of the road, laid on my back and laughed uncontrollably. Tears were rolling down my face as the young Troop Officer stood over me shouting, "Sort it!" But it didn't matter what he said, I couldn't get up.

2

HELLO N.I.

I looked down and there was nothing to see except rain. I could have been anywhere in the world, but the flight was scheduled to land at Aldergrove so I assumed it was down there somewhere.

Standing in the rain, I felt as though the whole world was staring at Jean and myself as we waited to be picked up. I hadn't a clue what the driver looked like and wondered if the opposition would approach us. It would be easy to spot us as newcomers with luggage and nervous looks on our faces.

"Jack?" came an inquiring Scouse voice.

I nodded to the five-foot-seven-inches-tall Scouser with the slim moustache.

"I'm parked over there," he said, jerking his thumb over his shoulder.

Jean and I breathed a sigh of relief and followed. We stowed the cases in the boot and jumped into the car.

"Jack," I said extending my hand. "This is my wife Jean."

"Scouse Wheels," he said, turning around to face us and shaking.

I asked him how he'd recognized me. He said that Stan Rigger (who had written to me and I knew from the past) had given him my description. I relaxed a little after the mention of a familiar name and settled down for the half-hour journey to Lisburn.

The camp entrance consisted of three check points operating on a tidal traffic basis: two in and one out at peak entry periods and two out and one in at peak exit periods. There was a concrete wall about ten feet tall and seven feet wide twenty yards down the road from the entrance. A sentry stood behind, peering through a slit at eye level, rifle lolling across his arms. Two soldiers patrolled up and down the road beyond the wall. VCPs (vehicle checkpoints) by the UDR and squaddies were frequent in this area.

It was late afternoon and no staff was available to do a handover/takeover of a quarter, so we'd been booked into the Sergeants' Mess for an overnight stay.

"Someone will collect you at half eight in the morning and take you to your quarter," said Scouse as he dropped us off.

The mess was no different to any other Sergeants' Mess. It had the usual entrance hall, a bar area and a large function room. There were walls with the usual pictures of the Queen and Prince Philip, photographs of teams or individuals who, through sporting prowess or helping the mess, were honoured by having their picture hung. The usual trophy cabinet was displaying cups, medals and shields from sporting victories. The usual regimental shields and plaques lined the walls, which had been presented by visiting units or individuals.

The next morning I stood outside the mess waiting for my transport to arrive at 8.30 and it was still raining. A car pulled up on the dot and out jumped a large, mustachioed, jolly giant with an infectious laugh.

"Robbie Wheels," he said with an outstretched arm.

"Jack Rigger," I said falling into the local jargon.

We shook hands firmly and were instant friends.

The quarter was on camp and I could have walked there in ten minutes. But, as I didn't know the way, they had laid on transport. Three minutes later I stepped out of the car and surveyed the house. It was the usual box-like, modern, characterless semi-detached located in a quiet tree-lined avenue on the edge of camp. Across the road was the wire-mesh perimeter fence. The usual detached garage stood at the side. Inside was like outside, neat and tidy. The back garden consisted of the usual blob of grass with trees at the bottom. The trees were tall with lots of low branches and served as a dividing line, giving a certain amount of privacy. The low branches were preventing light from entering the house. I knew I'd have to do something about them later.

The sound of a car pulling up drew me to the front of the house. A barrack warden stepped out of his car as I appeared. If everything went well the handover/takeover would only take an hour, so Robbie waited. I mentioned the trees to the warden just before he left. He said if they were to be cropped, it would have to be on a self-help basis due to lack of funds.

Our furniture was not due to arrive until the next day, so a get you in / get you out pack was left. It consisted of enough crockery and bedding to get you by until it did.

Robbie waited in the car outside the mess while I disappeared and then reappeared with Jean and the cases.

"Robbie, Jean. Jean, Robbie," I said, but shouldn't have bothered. They were firing witticisms at each other like long-lost friends and completely ignored me.

"See you soon," said Robbie, dropping off the last case for us.

We toiled at unpacking again and only realized late in the afternoon that we needed to buy things. The shop on camp was closed so we decided to venture out to some local shops. There was an unusual smell I'd noticed the day we had arrived and I continuously sniffed as we walked. The smell hung in the air no matter where we went and I tried to put a name to it. It suddenly hit me. Sulphur! I looked up at the relentless exodus of smoke rising lazily from the chimneys in vertical plumes and gave Jean a dig.

"What did we forget to put on the shopping list?" I said, pointing upwards.

We turned left and left again. A line of shops came into view beyond a large patch of grass. There was a newsagent, clothes shop, butchers, grocers, fish and chip shop and a hardware store. It was the grocers first. Then the hardware store for a small bag of coal. We were both very nervous at our first outing and we kept glancing over our shoulders. Just to be sure to be sure! We were glad of the relative security of the house when we got back.

A third member of Wheels picked me up the next morning and took me in to work. I stood beside him as he pressed a button on the left-hand side of an anonymous door. A camera relayed a picture of us on to a monitor in the ops room. The Bleeps (Member of the Royal Signals) watched.

"Who's that with you, Geordie?" came a crackly voice from a speaker microphone situated above the button.

"The new rigger," he replied.

A buzzing noise indicated the electronic door lock was energizing. We went in. Voices got louder as we walked down the corridor and we practically bumped into their owners as we turned a corner. Stan Rigger stood facing me and as he looked up a big smile spread across his face.

"Jack, how are you?" he asked.

We shook and fell into the usual conversation of what we'd been doing since the last time we'd met. That was in the early eighties; we were both instructors then and were teaching telecommunications at Catterick. He was heading back there having been promoted to Warrant Officer Class Two. I'll never forget the day he walked into the rest room at Catterick with a two-inch-wide red mark running down his forehead directly above his nose. Somebody had to ask the inevitable, "How did you get that?"

We'd been wiring up a classroom together so we could teach trainees line-testing. Stan had decided to Hilti-gun pins into the steel frame of the building so that we could run wires from the pins to test points and provide a common earth. He had wrapped a wire around the first pin and had tried to solder the wire to the pin with a small soldering iron, but the heat from the iron dissipated into the steel girder. The effect was that the pin and wire could not reach the right temperature to melt the solder. He went to the stores and withdrew the biggest soldering iron he could find, but it was still not working. He had pressed the soldering iron onto the pin as hard as he could, trying to force the heat in. It was whilst he was leaning forward to check the pin that he had acquired the red mark. The iron slipped and smacked him on the forehead!

"The Pronto," said Stan pointing to the person next to him.

"Roy," said Roy, extending his arm and giving a firm shake. His hand was tough-skinned and calloused and his shoulder-length hair surrounded his weather-beaten face. Definitely not a desk person.

"Paul YoS," (Yeoman of Signals – a yeoman deals with the

control and configuration of radio networks) said the man dressed in a dark business suit collar and tie who now leaned forwards. His hand was moist and the shake podgy. His mouth seemed to turn down at the right-hand side in what I assumed was an attempted smile, but finished up a small sneer. Below the sneer were two double chins. Definitely a desk person, one who could easily become fat but kept it in check by regular dieting.

The fourth person was not very forthcoming.

"Jim FoS," (Foreman of Signals – deals with the technical side i.e., the repair of equipment) said Stan, pointing to Jim.

He was slow to bring his hand up. It was as though he felt he was doing me a favour. The handshake was a quick squeeze and release. His body mannerisms were slightly rigid and when he spoke it was through partly clenched teeth.

"Got work to do," he said in a cockney accent. He then walked into his office and sat down. The YoS excused himself and followed. Roy looked at me and whispered, "The FoS is an ignorant bastard."

"I've already guessed that," I said, tuning in.

Arriving in a new unit is always a pain. It consists of being whisked around the relevant departments and being introduced to loads of new faces, half of which you forget right away. Stan gave me an outline of the morning. I had to book in to all departments and have an arrival interview with the Commanding Officer. He was the only person we called Sir. My furniture was arriving in the afternoon. Stan knew and had taken it into account.

"Come on. Spooks first," (Member of the Intelligence Corps) he said.

The spook induction covered the usual security brief, i.e. whatever happens or is said in this unit stays in this unit. Be alert at all times. Report any suspicious characters. He went on to say, because of my role in The Unit, that I would have to have a telephone installed at home, pay the bill and then be reimbursed and that the number would be ex-directory. It didn't mean much in Northern Ireland. BT had had all their ex-directory files stolen and they couldn't find out who'd done it, the spook told me. The more I learned the more I was gob-smacked by the situation.

After being spooked, I wandered back down to the Ops room to find Stan. A couple of bleeps sat monitoring radio channels as I walked in. They looked up and nodded and I nodded back. Stan must have been sitting in the YoS's office opposite the ops room when he saw me arrive.

"Ready for the next one?" he asked over my shoulder.

He took me down the corridor, turned right, then left into another corridor and extended his arm into the pay office.

"When you've finished here go next door and arrange an interview with the boss," he said before disappearing again.

Fifteen minutes to sort pay details, then next door. James Admin took my next of kin details, children's details, address here, address in the UK, car details, which side I dressed, how often did I shit and all the other personal information that is required to bare your soul for Queen and country. At the beginning of my Army career it used to really get up my nose, but after a few years you realize it has to be done.

James leaned forward to press a button on an antiquated intercom system, but before pressing he looked up.

"Stan's ordered a new intercom but hasn't had time to install it yet. I'd appreciate it if you could give it some priority," he said, then pressed the button.

"Yes."

"The new Rigger's in my office Sir. Could you see him now for arrival interview?"

"Send him in."

James stood, looked at me and inclined his head towards the door. It was down the corridor, turn right, then right again up another corridor. I'd only been here five minutes and I was already sick of corridors. I followed until he stopped outside the boss's office. He knocked and walked in. Holding the door open he announced, "Jack Rigger Sir."

The boss stood up as the door closed behind me and pointed to a chair facing his desk. He leaned across, shook my hand and welcomed me to the unit.

He came across as a very warm, caring and compassionate person. He explained how working in this unit could create a lot of pressure and that sometimes trivial matters seemed enormous. However, if I ever had any problems I was to speak to somebody. I liked him. My eye caught a photograph behind him. It was the usual end-of-course photograph where all the students posed in regimental fashion, standing up, arms folded in all the rows behind the front row, front row seated with arms extended in straight lines, hands on knees and backs bolt upright. This photograph was different. Everyone had their left hand covering their face so nobody could be recognized.

"If there are any problems my door's always open," he reassured.

It was getting on for twelve when I asked Stan if there was anything else lined up. There wasn't. I popped my head into the FoS and YoS's office.

"See you tomorrow."

The FoS looked up, grunted and then looked down. Roy's words went through my mind.

"Come in and collect a bleeper tomorrow," said the YoS. "You'll be on permanent call."

I told Jean about closing the curtains before switching on the lights. I also told her a telephone would be installed (that went with the job) and that contractors would be coming round to blast-proof the windows. This consisted of sticking large sheets of thick cling-foil to the inside of the windows to prevent shards of glass flying around if a bomb went off. As I was speaking to Jean a large removal van pulled up outside our quarter. Three men alighted from the van. They peered nervously through the perimeter fence and huddled together for security. I went out to greet them.

"Cuppa lads?"

"Best thing we've heard all day," said the driver to his two mates.

Jean, stood at the door, overheard and disappeared into the kitchen as I asked how the journey over had gone. The driver couldn't wait and the words gushed out of his mouth while he frowned heavily and continued peering through the perimeter fence. The driver said they'd been followed all the way from the port to just down the road. They were rattled but felt safer now they'd reached their destination, I didn't tell him how I felt. I asked them where they were staying tonight and they looked at me as though I was some space cadet.

"On camp, it's the only safe place." I felt exposed.

It was late February and it was dark before they'd finished. Climbing into their cab they continued to peer around and fidget. The van tail-lights disappeared around the corner, then the darkness and silence fell. It was as though a heavy mantle had been hovering above me, waiting to fill the hole that was left by the van.

I looked around and watched curtains that had been made to twitch by the sound of the van still themselves. I thought about the neighbours tucked away in their warm homes. I knew it wouldn't be long before they'd be knocking on our door to welcome us, but at that moment they seemed a thousand miles away. Solitude prevailed and the feeling of being alone drowned me.

We gazed on the disarray that goes with moving. We'd done it nine or ten times in the last eighteen years. We were use to it by now, but it never got any easier. A lot of hard work over the next few weeks was needed before it would be comfortable. The house was silent and filled with gloom as though a ghost lingered, so I decided to dig out the telly. First, I checked the list of what each box contained then I retrieved a screwdriver from one of the suitcases.

The light in the garage wasn't working and it was pitch black. There was no way I was going to the shops again, so I dug out my lighter. Holding it up, I began moving the twenty-two boxes one by one from one side of the garage to the other. I searched for box number eight as large looming shadows cascaded and flickered around the walls and ceiling. There were no traffic noises, chatter or stereos to be heard. Just the cold wind of February swirling some forgotten leaves around the garage floor. It was an eerie, lonely sound.

The road outside of camp curved where our house was. A car passed and its headlights shone directly into the garage as it swept towards me, totally illuminating the inside and silhouetting me. As it turned the bend, shadows swept swiftly from right to left leaving total darkness in their trail. I hesitated. Physically and mentally I pushed down the fear that was rising, then carried on. Dousing the light and working by touch, I found the screws with my fingers. I inserted the screwdriver and removed them, recovered the telly, locked the garage and went inside.

Voices leapt into all corners of the room, splashed into the hall and kitchen and removed the ghost that had been lingering. We curled up on the settee, relaxing and letting the warm glow of the fire and brandy-laced coffee do their thing. Ten-thirty and we'd reached that stage where our bodies and minds were totally relaxed. The world was shut out and anything beyond the room didn't exist. I savoured the feeling a while longer, then gently shook Jean; she came round, yawning. I switched off the telly and the room continued to glow. It was going to be home for the next two years.

I closed the front door behind me, peered at the road outside of camp and forcefully made myself relax. It didn't work. Every three steps I took I looked right and glanced at the road. It was Thursday and Stan was outlining the programme of locations and procedures to me. He was flying out on Saturday morning, so the next two days would be hectic.

"Hang on, Stan, I've got to see Paul," I said spotting Paul going into his office

"Good morning, Paul. Can I have a bleeper?"

"Hi, Jack," he said, opening his right-hand drawer.

"There are two modes of signal acknowledgement," he said. "A loud bleep which is no good as you don't know where you'll be when it goes off, or vibrator mode."

"Is there a choice of shape and colour for the girls?" I asked, smiling. I took the bleeper from him and headed for the door.

"Hang on, Jack." I turned and there he was, holding out the inevitable pen to sign for the piece of kit. How could I forget!

Stan ran through the procedure. Names, route, destination, time, call sign and task were written into the booking-out book. A radio receiver in the shape and size of a hearing aid was next, and then it was squeeze past two bleeps, grab my 9mm Browning pistol and fill two magazines.

"There isn't much fire power in a Browning so we take a support weapon," said Stan. "There are two kinds, a Heckler and Koch 53 and an MP5."

The MP5 had a higher rate of rpm (rounds per minute). It was easier to handle with the shorter barrel. It also had a larger magazine than the HK and was favoured by most of the lads. Stan pulled back the cocking mechanism and checked the chamber. Gun cleared, he took me to one side and ran me through the actions: load, unload, rate of fire lever, safety catch and cocking mechanism. Familiarization over, we filled the two mags that were taped together for fast mag change. He grabbed a civvie holdall from under a shelf and placed the MP5 and two smoke grenades inside. Zipped up, we set off for Wheels with Brownings tucked into our belts and jumpers pulled over them.

"Always keep the weapons out of sight when in civvies," he emphasized. "The security forces might mistake you for opposition."

Robbie and Scouse Wheels were in their office, so we had a quick chat. Stan declined the offer of coffee and asked for a car.

"The silver Montego," Robbie said, throwing over a bunch of keys.

"We've got it for the next two days, haven't we?" said Stan, catching the keys and confirming.

"There's always a pool of cars to choose from," he said as we walked across the car park. "Just in case one gets compromised. If there's a lot of special kit installed a re-spray and plate change can be arranged."

Stan cocked his 9mil, applied the safety and placed it on the seat under his thigh. I copied. Smoke grenades were stowed in the glove compartment and magazine placed on the support weapon, which was then secreted away in the door compartment. My leg hid the support weapon, but, to be sure, I rested my arm across it. Once the radio was checked we were off.

Driving through Belfast I kept leaning to my right and glancing in the nearside rear-view mirror.

"Try and relax, I've got my eye on things behind," said Stan. I tried, it wasn't easy.

Today would consist of visiting two of the dets (detachments), South and East. It was tight security at East, but no problem as Stan

30

introduced himself to the unseen faces watching the camera monitor. Access granted, we entered and met the two resident techs who serviced, repaired and sometimes installed the radio fits in the cars.

I'd noticed the radio fit in the Montego and quizzed Stan about it, as none of the equipment could be seen. The bulk of it was installed in the boot with the microphone hidden on the dashboard. The receivers were in our ear, away from the car door to reduce the risk of them being spotted. Antennae have to be cut to a certain length to enable them to receive the correct frequency and this presented a problem. An unusual antenna would have to be mounted on the car and it would stand out. We got round this by producing the correct antennae to transmit the frequency and then we disguised it into the same antenna model as the car it was fitted to. The transmit button was positioned on, or near, the gear stick where no unusual movement could be detected when it was being pressed. One of the techs, Paddy, was leaving the Army soon. Paddy was off to the States where he was setting up an antiques business. He was busy buying antiques when home on leave and his aim was to fill a container, ship it over to the states and sell the antiques. He'd already taken out a lease on a shop in Boston to begin one week after his discharge, so he had a tight schedule. I asked him how he was going to replenish his stock. He said he hadn't worked that out yet, but that he would. He had a heart of gold and we wished him all the luck in the world at his farewell.

Paddy used to be at HQ, but was moved to East after fitting a radio into the boss's car. Apparently the boss was driving home after the radio fit on a dark night and decided to try it out. He switched the radio on and all the lights went out. It was the radio or lights, not both together. Paddy was moved.

I was introduced to the Pronto and Sunray (the boss of the det.). Then it was a walk round taking in the intercom system, cable routes and antenna configurations.

South was a much larger complex. After clearing through the security measures, we drove around two helicopters and parked inside a huge building. The building housed the support staff, operators (soldiers from any unit who are trained in surveillance techniques) and members of the Troop. Once again, I was introduced to the Pronto and Sunray who told us the techs were still in bed as they'd been working all night on a rush job. We decided to have lunch and catch them later.

There weren't many people in the canteen as most operations were carried out at night. So people slept by day. I strolled up to the empty hot plate and ordered a cheese and mushroom omelette while Stan ordered a burger and chips.

"Burger and chips and one cheese omelette," shouted the cook ten minutes later.

"Over here," I shouted from the table.

The cook looked at me and started laughing.

"There's no waiter service here," he said, putting the dinners on the hotplate.

"I'll get em," said Stan. He came back and plonked the meals on the table, sat down and started scoffing. He picked his chips up with one hand and his burger with the other, and got stuck in. I asked him where the knives and forks were and a grin broke over his face.

"Oh," he said, "I forget to tell you. You need your own knives and forks."

I looked down at my omelette and my mouth watered. I thought about the knives and forks and then decided to go ahead without them. I picked up the omelette with my fingers and got stuck in. The omelette was a little runny in the middle and bits dribbled out and splattered on the plate as I ate it. After four or five bites it was getting a bit ridiculous with egg smeared all around my mouth and running down my arms below my sleeves. All through this Stan was laughing and other diners who had come in were slagging me off. Even the chef reappeared to have a dig and a laugh. Three-quarters of the way through the omelette, the egg, running down my arms, was nearing my elbow and I couldn't take any more. It felt like slime creeping slowly down, congealing on the way. I dashed out with egg on my face while holding my arms up and headed for the heads (nautical term for toilet) with the diners and chef jeering. When I got there, I needed to pull up my sleeves but my hands were covered in egg. Keeping my arms up, I bowed my head, gripped a sleeve with my teeth and pulled it up. I shouldn't have bothered as the egg on my face went all over my sleeve anyway, so I pulled the other sleeve up with my egg-splattered hand. Turning on the cold tap, I washed my arms, hands and face then tried to locate the paper towels. No such luck, so I went to a toilet and dragged off a stream of bog paper.

Stan was sucking his fingers when I went back in. He looked up as I neared the table and that grin appeared again.

"I enjoyed that," he said, rubbing it in. "Come on. We'll see if the techs are up."

We opened their doors quietly and peered in. They were sleeping.

"You'll catch them later," Stan said.

He showed me round the Det, pointing out the communications systems and cable runs, and then we headed back.

We parked the Montego and went into the tech workshops where Stan introduced me to three techs. The one with fair hair and angelic choirboy appearance was Roy Tech. Looking at him, I wondered how he coped with the demands of this job. I would be out on many a job with Roy and he proved to be highly professional with a lot of balls, as were most of the people I was to meet.

Stan Tech was next. (You could have the same name as long as you had a different job specification, i.e. rigger or tech.) We shook hands and held each other's gaze momentarily. His eyes gave off an impish look. When you coupled this with his black straight hair that fell over his forehead and his five feet seven inches height, you were immediately reminded of a naughty schoolboy. He didn't know what the future held. He was due to get his hair parted not once, but twice.

Frank Tech was the one always copying blue movies. This went with his black hair slicked to one side, and large nose under which a moustache grew.

We laughed and talked about the places we'd been to and the people we knew. Twenty minutes later Stan said, "Come on. I'll show you the riggers' shack."

He slipped me a bunch of keys as we walked towards a large

garden shed at the side of the tech workshops and he said, 'They're yours. I won't be needing them again."

Tools lay on top of a bench next to a plastic open-fronted box which had drawers containing connectors, solder, screws, wall plugs and all the other small paraphernalia that goes with rigging. Folded dipole antennae, ropes and climbing belts hung from walls. Long, thin, end-fed whip antennae rested across the two horizontal roof beams and coils of thin coaxial cable were piled in corners.

"That's yours as well," Stan said, peering out of the window and pointing to thicker coaxial cable snaked around large drums which sat on a grass verge. He ran through the procedure for ordering stores. Then we locked up and walked to the ops room to book in.

"Same time tomorrow," I enquired. Stan nodded.

Jean was cooking something for dinner as I walked in and I couldn't resist leaning over her shoulder and sniffing the contents of the pan.

"That smells good," I said, as my hands started to wander. I squeezed her bum and she gave me a playful slap and pushed me away, so I wandered into the lounge and sat down.

A couple of pictures had been hung on the walls and the place was looking better already. We talked loudly to each other while I took my boots off and Jean told me that two of the neighbours had popped in for a chat. She said they coped with the situation by keeping themselves to themselves and never visiting any bars off camp. They did a lot of reading and invited each other round to their houses for a game of Trivial Pursuit, or whatever, while taking in a few beers. We swopped the days events, then ate. I did some more unpacking, then settled in. The house had belongings scattered all around. We ignored them, put our feet up and relaxed.

Stan had booked us out, got the weapons and retrieved the Montego by the time I got in. The journey to North detachment would take about three hours. He didn't want to be late back. I asked if it was OK if I drove. He didn't have a problem with that. The driver's seat needed adjusting, as Stan was a little taller. The leg room was fine but the tilt needed to come forward a notch. The backrest fell away when I pulled the tilt lever and I thought the spring mechanism had gone. I reached behind and tried to lift it, but it wouldn't budge.

"The seat's jammed," I told Stan.

I had to get into the back of the car to lift it but even then it was difficult. "What's inside this, Stan?"

"Same as the doors," he said. "Armour plating."

It took the two of us to lift the seat into the upright position. Then Stan had to stay in the back and hold it while I adjusted. It wasn't raining but the sky was grey and leaden. It depressed the soul and we drove in silence for the first half-hour.

We came across some road works and I noticed a subtle difference in the wording: England – ROAD WORKS SLOW; Ireland – SLOW ROAD WORKS.

I broke the silence. "Had any tight scrapes?"

"Not really," he said. "I've had a few twitches where I was in a certain place in the morning and there had been a bomb or a shooting in the afternoon, but I haven't been involved in an incident."

We drove on. None of us was saying much and none of us caring about saying much. It was just a journey. We passed a home-made sign at the side of the road: FRESH PETROL 200YDS. I'm still trying to work that out.

North det was on the same lines as South and East det. It was surrounded by a high steel-shuttered perimeter fence and festooned with security cameras. It was also a pretty similar set-up inside. It didn't take long to run through the comms side of things. Going through the intercom system reminded me about the one in HQ.

"Where's the equipment for the intercom in HQ?" I asked.

Stan described a small storeroom in the adjoining corridor between the two main corridors.

"I felt that was the best place to install the equipment, so I've stored it in there," he said.

The storeroom was ideally situated for the cable runs. I nodded in agreement. He pointed to a building with a small pond at the side.

"That's the bar," he said. "Watch out when you come and stay overnight. Most new visitors get thrown in the pond and everybody pisses in it. Have you noticed the big fat clerk at HQ?" he continued. "When he came up it took four of them to carry him out of the bar and throw him in. He cracked three ribs when he hit the water. It was winter and frozen solid."

We arrived back at half-three after another scintillating journey and made our way to the ops room. The ops room had a party spirit to it. Soldiers were slagging each other off, catcalling and laughing. Someone shouted, "The bar's open," and there was a mass exodus as people stampeded down the corridor to the bar at the other end of the building. I was giving the bar a miss tonight. I thanked Stan for his help. I also wished him all the best on his next posting, shook his hand and once again we parted. I walked out of the office door and was pleasantly surprised to see an old mate standing there.

"Fancy meeting you, Dave. What're you doin' over here?"

"I've just been posted into three nine brigade to replace Del," he said, pointing to Del, who was standing next to him. "Del, this is Jack," said Dave.

Del stepped forward and we shook. "This is Sheila and we've just got engaged," he said, winking at the bubbly blonde next to him and giving her a hug.

Del had re-toured and was now coming to the end of his fourth successive year. He had two days to push. We shook hands for the last time. He would die next day.

"Are you leaving with him?" I asked Sheila.

"No, I've got another six months left," she said. "But I'm counting the days."

Dave had arrived on the same day as me and we talked about our feelings and sensations on arrival. We laughed together as we expressed the same fears. It would be the last time we laughed together.

"I was glad the driver wasn't delayed."

"So was I."

"I'd been told not to get into a black cab."

"Me too." I heard the office door open behind me and I watched Del raise his head and at the same time lift his left wrist up and peer at his watch.

"You're late," he said to the person behind me. I turned and watched Roy stroll over with a big grin on his face. Roy stopped at the side of me and rested one hand on the handle bars and one hand on the saddle of the bicycle he was pushing.

Del and Roy had known each other for years and were the best of mates.

"Got anything on tomorrow?" Roy asked Del.

"Yeah. We're off to Woodbourne," he said, flicking his thumb from Dave to himself.

"We've got to install a couple of telephone extensions."

"It might be worth you going with them, Jack," said Roy. "We work out of there quite a lot."

"We're leaving at nine. If you want to come along, it's no problem," said Del.

"Where are you leaving from?" I asked.

"Three nines compound."

I thought about it then said, "If I'm not there, go without me."

"Well," shouted Roy.

"Well," shouted Del. "The bar is waiting. Let's go."

"Catch you later, Dave, and good luck with your next posting, Del," I said as they started to walk up the road.

Saturday mornings were a pretty relaxed affair. We often discussed the previous and forthcoming operations. We would work on ways to improve procedures, as well as the technical side of things, and prioritize them. No matter how much you planned it, it never went accordingly, due to the amount of immediate requests we received.

Roy was in the kitchen having a coffee with a couple of the Bleeps and Brian when I walked in. There was an awful smell of garlic. It was so bad it made my nose twitch and my stomach churn. This was a regular Saturday morning feature of Roy's. He always got pissed on Friday nights. He would always cycle home and finish up in privet hedges. He would also get an incredible urge for garlic and scoffed it by the clove when he got home.

"I always leave my bike just inside the front door," he said. "I came out of the bar one night and it had gone." His conversation was aimed at me, so was his breath. I was taking in shallow breaths, holding them for as long as I could. I tried not to inhale.

37

I leaned backwards and put as much distance between us as possible. I tried not to make it obvious, so as not to embarrass him. He carried on.

"I thought I might have left it outside. I'd looked around, but couldn't find it. Then I thought," he said, pointing a finger in the air like some brainwave had hit him, "Somebody's hidden it. So I looked inside the building, but I still couldn't find it." He stretched his arms forwards in front of himself and held his palms upwards while pushing his head backwards to show his frustration. "In the end I thought sod it and headed back to the bar."

My stomach was really churning and I broke into a sweat. I couldn't believe something could taste so nice on its way down and smell so fucking awful on its way up. Get a bloody move on Roy, I thought. I can't stand much more of this.

"They were all expecting me back, and started laughing when I walked in," Roy continued. "Stan shouted to me, 'Lost something, Roy?' 'Alright,' I said, 'where is it?' 'Go outside the front door and look up,' he told me. I went back outside and looked up," he said, leaning forward to deliver the punch line. I couldn't take any more. I had to step back. Roy stepped forward. I had to turn away. He grabbed my jacket, pulled me close and said, "It was swinging at the top of the mast, one hundred and twenty feet up."

He took deep breaths and expelled each word up my nose. I pushed him away, then turned my back on him. I gagged and nearly puked. My stomach stopped churning and instead started heaving. The garlic was so strong I was in danger of having my smell sense burnt out.

The sound of laughter dragged Jim FoS out of his office. He stood there with that 'do not disturb' look on his face. There was tension in his body. His arms were straight at his sides and his jaw was clenched.

"Good morning Jim," I said.

He turned on his heel, gave me the cursory grunt and went back into his office. I hunched my shoulders, raised my palms up and smiled at Roy. He mouthed, "Ignorant Twat."

The intrusion killed the conversation stone dead.

"What are you doing this morning?" asked Brian.

"I've got two options," I told him. "I can install the intercom or go over to Woodbourne with Del from three nine."

"It's a nice day. I know which one I'd choose," said Brian, walking out of the kitchen sipping coffee. It was a nice day. I'd rather be out than in anytime. Should I go with Del and Dave, or should I install the intercom? I pondered, drawn by the chance to escape the indoor, pulled back by the urgency of the intercom. It turned out to be one of the most critical decisions of my life!

The morning passed quickly, as it does when you're busy. I strolled home in the weak sunshine. I thought about the boring afternoon that lay ahead, unpacking boxes! I was on my fourth box when the phone rang – our first call. Only two people knew our number. Our daughter Belinda, and work. It was probably a wrong number.

"Hello," I said.

"It's Paul YoS," he said.

"Have you been watching the Tele?"

"No."

There was an intake of breath. A short pause. Then he came straight out with it. "They've just killed two of our lads from three nine. There's nothing we can do. Don't come in."

My mind was frozen. Then it began to race. "Was it Del and Dave?" I asked.

"Yes, do you know them?"

"It doesn't matter," I said.

I stopped breathing. My heart stopped beating. The world stood still. I turned and faced Jean. She knew something was wrong. When I told her she sucked in deeply. She had known Dave and visibly shook, then went pale. It was as though someone had punched her in the stomach. I sat her down and made her a coffee laced with brandy. Her colour began to return and she calmed.

About six that evening the phone rang. Jean answered.

"Calm down, Belinda. Your Dad's all right. Jack, speak to your daughter," she said, holding out the phone.

"Hello Belinda, how are you?"

I couldn't understand a word she was saying she was talking so fast.

"Calm down, Belinda. What's wrong?"

She was sobbing now.

"I've been trying to get hold of you since the IRA funeral. They said the people killed were probably Royal Signals. You've been engaged all day. I thought it was you."

No names had been released. Everyone with a relative serving in Northern Ireland would have been trying to get through. Belinda was pouring out the words, releasing the tension inside her. I listened and waited for her to calm. She began to slow down. I talked. It was about nothing in particular. Just talk, until she calmed.

"I'll pass you onto your mum," I said. "She's dying to have a word."

Jean was right next to me. She was there all the time. I passed the handset over and disappeared into the garage. Only ten boxes left. I'd be glad to see the back of them.

I was making my way down the corridor to the ops room on Monday morning when Brian came round the corner. He stopped dead in his tracks, cup halfway to his mouth, and stared. I looked down and said,

"There's nothing hanging out is there?"

"Your dead," he said, still holding the same pose.

"What gave you that idea?" I asked.

"I heard you say on Saturday morning that you might go out with Del. Then I heard Del and a new guy had run into the IRA funeral. I thought it was you."

"It was Del's replacement that was with him. I decided to give it a miss," I said.

"Did you hear how they found out about it?" asked Brian.

"No."

Brian continued, "They'd radioed in to say they were leaving Woodbourne and were heading back to Lisburn," said Brian. "And that was the last three nine heard of them. The next thing three nine knew was Sheila [Del's fiancée] asking for the orderly officer. She was really distressed and the orderly officer had to wait for her to calm down. 'They've just topped Del and Dave,' she told the orderly officer. Can you imagine that? The orderly officer said, 'Are you sure? We haven't heard anything.' 'I've just seen it on TV,' she told him. 'They drove into the IRA funeral. I was watching it.'" Watching Del and Dave get beaten up. Watching them get murdered. "The orderly officer started to check around," continued Brian. "Reports were coming in about an incident at the funeral. The orderly officer put two and two together and made four." People react differently to bad news. Some quietly accept it while others become aggressive. Brian quietly accepted it. No wonder; I found out later he was on his eleventh consecutive year in the Province.

The kitchen was sombre when I walked in. People sipped coffee and whispered. Roy had been close to Del and it hit him hard. His body was there, but his mind elsewhere. I tried lighthearted conversation with him, but gave up. Their car was recovered that afternoon. There was a bullet hole in the floor on the passenger side. Dave might have been trying to frighten the crowd off. He may have accidentally discharged when he was cocking his weapon. We'll never know.

Driving home that day I was angry. No, not angry. FURIOUS. I had never been so furious in the whole of my life. I wanted to shout. Hit somebody. Ram somebody's car. But I held it in check. My chest felt heavy and a coldness devoured me. A small chink of ice, roughly the size of an ice cube, appeared in my chest. It was as though I'd undergone surgery and had an implant inserted. The feeling was so real and present that I had to rub it. It burned brightly and strongly, in a cold sort of way.

The YoS came round a few days later. He took the names of anyone who wanted to attend their funeral. The chunk of ice in my chest glowed brightly. It seemed to increase in size by a fraction. When he asked me, I rubbed it. I wondered if it was alive. Later I realized it was. It wasn't a physical living thing, but an emotional living thing. I fed it on anger and hate, and it grew by the day. An odd picture came into my mind. It was me, yelling and screaming at the funeral. I would have broken down. I knew I would.

"No thanks Paul. I'll give it a miss," I told him.

"Range day this Saturday," Brian told everyone. "You have to be there," he emphasized.

We sat on a hillside, smoking, chatting, and waiting for Dave RSM to begin. He went over Del and Dave's incident and told us all he knew. He filled in the blank bits. He finished and he was quiet. We were quiet. It reminded me of the two-minute silence on the eleventh day at the eleventh hour. The two-minute silence was broken by a screech. A screech from a seagull hovering above which had a staring left eye.

One seagull.

One lone seagull.

Odd there should be only one at this beach location.

Very odd.

"If," said Dave, breaking the silence and gaining our attention, "you ever do get caught in a crowd situation, grab a hostage. By the hair. Preferably a woman. Hold a gun to her head. Threaten to shoot her." He delivered the instructions in short sharp sentences. An economy of words. Ramming the points home.

"Walk away from the situation. With the hostage. There's always the gobby one. The one who incites the rest. If you feel you are in a no-win situation take the gobby one out. It usually works."

There was a ten-minute break, then it was Brian's turn.

"Any road block you come across that is manned by armed civvies *must* be classed as hostile," he began. "Two operators will now give you a demonstration on how to deal with this situation."

The meeting point had been selected well. It gave us a clear view of a road that ran down the centre of a small valley which had been purpose-built for this type of situation. Brian waved to the car in the distance and said to us, "Watch."

To begin with it was difficult to tell whether the car was moving. The first thing we saw was dust being pumped up from under the front of the car. The dust hung in the windless valley. It formed a ball and got bigger and bigger. It enveloped the car. The car drove out of the ball and sucked part of it with it. It raised more dust as it travelled forward. It reminded me of a horizontal nuclear explosion. First the ball, then the plume as the ball rose. This was the reverse. The ball stayed static and the plume lengthened as the car shot forward. The car sped into the S bend in the track. It drifted slightly left in the first bend. Then right in the next bend. It came out the other side. The brakes slammed on as a target popped up in front and to the right. Dust rose again to form another ball. The dust now resembled an unbalanced dumbbell with a large weight on one end and a smaller one at the other. An automatic weapon opened up from inside the car. Glass showered the bonnet and dust kicked up around the target. The driver exited and dived to the side. He stood up and, zig-zagging, ran fifteen paces back. He stopped, turned around, knelt and put covering fire onto the target. The passenger exited. He ran back thirty paces, stopped, turned around, knelt and poured covering fire onto the target. They leap-frogged each other, skirmishing until out of range. They stood up, hid their weapons and walked away.

Brian talked us through it. He explained it step by step.

"Any questions?" he asked. There was silence.

"OK then, who's first?" he asked.

Two young Bleeps, Tom and John, jumped up, both eager and ready to drive a car fast and open up with automatic weapons. They ran toward the start point. "Calm down," Brian shouted after them. They didn't. They sat there, faces clearly visible through the empty windscreen. The engine revved up. They were rarin' to go. Brian waved. The wheels spun, dust rose and they shot forward. They crunched the gears between first to second. A cheer came from the hillside. Laughter broke out. The first in many a day. There were smiles on our faces and we were happy. A touch of happiness that I'll never forget. We could see them leaning forward, urging the car on. The engine was fully revved in second. They slipped into the first bend and drifted across. We held our breath as two wheels dropped into the ditch at the side of the road and the car tilted slightly. Out of the ditch and back on the road. A 'Yo' emerged from the crowd and we were buzzing and laughing. They came into the second bend, still at full revs. Same again as they drifted across. Two wheels into the ditch. Car tilts slightly, their eager expressions now changing to one of concern, both realizing they'd overdone it, but too late to do anything. They tried to get back on the road but didn't quite make it. They slipped back in again. A bit more tilt and over they went. We just stood on the hillside, howling and laughing. Nobody rushing to check them. We made our way down, dragged them out and gave them shit until their faces glowed with embarrassment. It would be a long time before they lived this one down.

"I don't normally bring a spare car," said Chris Spanner (REME). "Lucky I did this time." He drove the low-loader to the start point and dropped off a good car, then he came and picked up the duff one. Two members from sub-unit Seven strolled over to the start point. They jumped into the good car and waited until we'd settled on the hillside again.

Stan had introduced me to both of them. We'd got on well, which was a good thing. The smaller one at six feet tall and shoulders to match, Rob Seven, was to become my future son-in-law. They had been in The Province for about twelve months and it showed in their mannerisms and attitude. They were experienced soldiers.

They drove forward. Drifted through the S bend. Slammed the brakes on as a target appeared on the left and opened up with automatic fire. Glass was still spraying the bonnet as Rob exited and ran back fifteen paces. He knelt and put down covering fire for the driver. The driver exited the car and ran back thirty paces. As he knelt down another target popped up on the right and in front of the car. Brian was enjoying himself this morning. He loved to catch people out. Rob saw it immediately. He turned and redirected his fire. We had an excellent view. We could see his rounds smacking into the road behind the car, little dust pouches rising above the points of impact. He was firing low. He noticed and adjusted by raising his weapon. A line of holes riddled the rear wing. The rear window disintegrated. Then he found the target. They carried on skirmishing and got out of range, hid their weapons and walked away. They returned to the car and we joined them. More shit flew as we told them that they would have to replace the rear tyre they'd blown out. Rob opened the boot, looked in and said, "Spanners, this is one for you," then walked away.

"He's shot up the spare as well," said Chris, peering in.

We should have been there for four hours. We were there for two.

Wherever you are, control gets to know everything.

44

"Tom and John. Hear you're taking up stock car racing," came over the radio. It was straight out of the blue. Totally unexpected, we roared. It was quickly followed by, "Want to borrow some car filler, Rob?"

We left in much better spirits than we'd arrived.

3

OUT AND ABOUT

Del and Dave's funerals generated a lot of media interest. Roy had been worried about his face being seen on TV as he was going to the funeral. This would have compromised his position in the Province, especially on covert operations. I didn't realize it was him when he walked in the day after the funeral. His moustache was gone and his long hair was shorn and dyed. His wife found it very amusing and thought she had a new man.

Two jobs came up. Fit a new antenna at Warren Point police station and sort a fault out at Dungannon police station. It was my first time out alone. I checked and double-checked the OOB (Out Of Bounds) map and selected a route. I memorized it. I made up a route card and selected alternative routes, just in case. Then I went to find Roy.

"Roy, where are the police stations at Warren Point and Dungannon?"

"Just head for the masts sticking up in the centre of town. You can't go wrong," he said.

Down at the riggers' shack I ran off one hundred and twenty feet of coaxial feeder cable. I soldered a connector onto one end of the cable and then screwed the connector onto the antenna. I sealed the joint with self-amalgamating tape, then covered that with a grease-impregnated tape. Tested it, then coiled it up. Next came the transport. I checked the oil, water, battery, lights, tyre pressures and spare wheel on the Ford Transit, then tanked up. I loaded everything I needed plus all the things I thought I might need, just in case. I booked out. I withdrew my Browning, two smoke grenades and a support weapon. Then I checked the route and alternative routes again. Tickles of fear bubbled in my stomach as I cocked the Browning, applied the safety and put it on the seat under my thigh. I placed the support weapon on the passenger seat then covered it with my jacket. I was ready. Final radio check.

"Hello zero, this is zero seven."

"Go ahead seven."

"I'm leaving your location and going to my first location."

"You're leaving my location and going to your first location?"

Two bursts of squelch to confirm his message (press the radio transmit button to produce a squelch noise that is transmitted).

I drove down the A1 to Newry and picked up the A2 to Warren Point. Approaching Warren Point, I spotted the mast and headed for it. I hoped there wouldn't be a complicated one-way system.

"Hello zero, this is zero seven."

"Go ahead seven."

"I'll be at my location in approx five minutes. Can you let them know?"

"You'll be at your location in five minutes. I'll let them know."

Two bursts of squelch from me to confirm his message. I pressed a button on the support post of the steel gates and waited. People passed and stared. A small cover drew back at eye level and a policeman peered out. I passed my NI driving licence through. There was no driving licence inside the cover, just my ID.

I sat in the cab with the engine running waiting for the gate to fully open, then drove in. I parked below the mast, climbed out and peered up. There didn't seem to be any problems with regard to the climb. It was straightforward with no obstacles and there was a position at about eighty feet to site the antenna. The mast was slim and had horizontal and diagonal strengthening struts between the legs. The horizontal struts were about the same distance apart as rungs on a stepladder, so climbing would be easy. It was my first job and I wasn't quite sure what the score was. I explained what I was about to do to the desk sergeant.

"Don't go up until I've put a couple of mobile patrols out. I'd put a marksman on the roof if I had more manpower. Let me know when you're ready," he said.

I began preparing everything for the sprint up the mast. Which it would be. I laid the feeder cable out on the ground in snakes to prevent it from snagging. Then I threaded a zip tie through the hole on each of the two adjustable spanners, looped the zip ties and slipped the loops on to a carabenna on my belt. I placed a pair of cutters into my top pocket and hung a long pouch on a nylon cord around my neck. The pouch was filled with additional zip ties. I then zipped the antenna on to a second carabenna on my belt. To prevent the weight of the cable from pulling the joint apart, I looped the cable a couple of times and zipped the loops to the carabenna. The belt lay on the floor at the base of the mast. All I had to do was fasten it around my waist and climb. I went back into the police station and told the sergeant I was ready.

"Wait until I give the OK," he said.

I was standing at the base of the mast waiting when four constables came out of the station. They gave me a 'you're disturbing our tea break look' and got into their patrol cars. They drove to the gate and waited. The sergeant came out and opened the gate, closed it after them then disappeared back into the station.

I stood there mentally preparing myself. I waited for the sergeant and wished he would hurry. He appeared at the door and gave me the thumbs up, then disappeared back into the station. I looked up, took a deep breath, and climbed.

I was covered by the wall for the first thirty feet of the climb and the spanners attached to the carabenna jangled quietly and steadily. At thirty-five feet I was fully exposed. I moved faster now, much faster. The spanners were in tune with my movement. They jangled faster and louder, drawing attention. Eighty feet and stop. Belt off with slightly shaking hands. Mentally shut down and cut the world out. Unscrew the nuts on the U-bolts of the ring clamps. Remove the U-bolts from the ring clamps and put them in the top pocket of my overalls. Mental note to have the U-bolts unscrewed before climbing next time. Zip-tie cable to mast to prevent joint from being pulled apart. Hold antenna. Cutters out of top pocket. Cut zip ties holding antenna to carabenna. Place antenna in position. Begin clamping. If I drop a nut I'll have to go down for it. Another mental note. Carry spare nuts and spare U-bolt. I cross-threaded a nut, and cursed. I held the antenna with one hand and removed a spanner from the carabenna. Not easy with one hand. Sorted it. Replace spanner. All nuts on. Run nuts down threads and finger-tighten. Two hands free to remove spanner this time. Lock off nuts. Zip-tie feeder cable to the mast leg. Cutters out of top pocket. Cut excess off zip ties. Replace cutters. One thought at a time. Don't think about the next one until this one is done. Quick glance over Warren Point. All quiet. Undo belt. Down eight rungs. Stop. Leg between struts and down inside of mast. Tuck toe under opposite strut. Zip-tie cable to mast leg every four rungs. Cutters. Cut off excess. Replace cutters. Down eight rungs. The routine continued until I was below thirty feet. Then I fastened my belt around the mast and rested. Down to the bottom. Couldn't go into the station yet. My voice would be squeaky. Lit a fag. Had a rest. Walked into the station.

"I've finished," I told the desk sergeant.

He looked up, nodded and called in the patrols.

I poked the feeder through the cable entry duct, then I went into the garden shed at the base of the mast and pulled in the slack. Cut it to length and soldered it on to a connector, then tested. The techs would come along later with their equipment.

There was no stopping at roadside cafes for obvious reasons. It was lunch in the van, look relaxed, and nod to the returning patrols.

"Zero, this seven," I said.

"Go ahead seven."

"I'm leaving my first location and going onto my second."

"'You're leaving your first location and going onto your second?"

Two bursts of squelch from me to confirm his message. One burst would have meant no.

Finding the police station at Dungannon was as easy as finding the one at Warren Point. Head for the mast. It wasn't a mast but a tower. A mini-version of the one on the rigging course. Memories flooded back. I reported to the desk sergeant and told him what I was doing.

"Okay," he said, and carried on writing.

I waited, hoping for a marksmen and mobile patrols. He looked up.

"Is there anything else?"

"Well. It's the first time I've climbed at Dungannon. Are there any precautions I need to take?" I asked. He looked up and grinned.

"Yeah, keep ducking!"

I walked out with that dickhead feeling on me.

The records had said that the antenna was sited on the north-facing leg at ninety feet. Which was north? Climb up. Inch out on three inches of steel to a leg. Wrong one. Inch in and inch out again. Bingo!

Nine times out of ten the fault is water in the joint connecting the feeder to the antenna. I opened it and breathed a sigh of relief as water ran out. I wouldn't have to work late changing the feeder or antenna. I dried the inside of the joint, then let it hang in the breeze for a few minutes. I reconnected and waterproofed with the two tapes, then climbed down. Tested it with a meter and transmitted over it. Clear as a bell.

Roy Pronto was in the far corner of the bar with the techs and looked up as I walked in, calling me over.

"What do you want to drink?" he asked.

"Draught Guinness."

"Draught Guinness," he shouted to the barman over the noise and pointed to me.

"Draught Guinness coming up," shouted the barman.

I was caught completely unaware. Drinkers between the bar and me stepped to one side and created an empty corridor. The Guinness came hurtling towards my head.

I ducked. Tried an overhead catch, but missed. Roy picked up the Guinness and handed it to me. The whole bar was watching, and grinning. Guinness started to froth as I tore off the ring pull. I ducked. Brought the can up at the same time and started gulping. The flow began to subside and I smiled over the can. The crowd was losing interest until the compressed air capsule cracked. Black liquid shot up my nose making me cough and splutter. I moved the can away and kept my head bowed to allow nasal drainage, and raised my arm in submission. A cheer came from the crowd as I wiped my face on my jumper. Boy, did I need that drink. It had that extra rich flavour of the drink you've waited all week for. One of those knee-trembling, spine-tingling, finger-twitching ones.

I related my day's events. Warren Point and Dunganon with the 'keep ducking' bit. Not to be outdone, John Tech chipped in about the time he rolled a car. He said he was out with Steve Tech in bandit country when he took a bend too fast and rolled the car onto its roof.

"Steve and I were hanging upside down. We were both OK, but wondering what to do. The radio was out. We couldn't wander around with weapons in civvies and we didn't want to advertise our accents. If we stayed near the car and formed a defensive position it could be dodgy both ways with regards to the IRA or the Security Forces. In the end we decided to pretend we were unconscious. Weapons were lying around. We were hanging upside down, and a crowd started to gather," he continued.

"The crowd were talking to us. Trying to bring us round, as they didn't know whether we were IRA or Security Forces. We didn't want the shit kicked out of us so remained silent," he said. "The police arrived and moved the crowd back when they saw the weapons. One of them leaned in and began to talk to me. I opened my eyes and there was this upside-down copper. 'We're covert, get us out of this place,' I told him. The copper wanted to see my ID so I undid my belt and forgot I was upside down. I fell and banged my head on the roof of the car. We couldn't leave the car, so a green team (soldiers in uniform) arrived and guarded it until Wheels picked it up," he said.

"George, tell him about Strabane," said Roy.

George outlined Strabane for me.

"The police station there is in a state of continual rebuild. Getting the civvies to work there is a major problem. They can be easily followed and targeted," he said. "I was asked to put a camera up, and it was guaranteed you'd get shot at if you climbed. Green teams were everywhere that night. I even put cam cream on, which I'd never done before. Once at the top, I hauled up my vest. I put on night scopes and hung my HK within easy reach. There was more personal equipment than surveillance equipment," he laughed. "The work was really slow. Every two or three minutes I'd look up and scan. It was taking me so long I had to go back the next night to finish it." He started to laugh again. Took a swig of his beer. Hung the story out. He went on. "It was about three in the morning and a patrol was having a break at the gate. They were sipping tea and keeping warm. Then all I heard was, 'Look up there lads. There's someone up the mast'. I couldn't believe it," he said. "If the terrorists didn't know I was there before, they did now. So I shouted 'Cheers mate!' The next day I heard they'd blown up Strabane again. There was no way I was going through that again."

My day's jaunt felt small and insignificant after that. I didn't want to get too pissed as I was going shopping the next day. Now was a good time to leave.

Jean and I drove through lush green countryside to Knutts' Corner market. I reminded her of a couple of precautions. Don't talk near the car. Only whisper when we are walking round. Parking was not a problem as a couple of fields had been set aside. I turned into the first field and parked up. We walked across the road, Jean ducking slightly at my side. She was searching for cover against the chill March wind.

We melted into the crowd, trying to look relaxed whilst remaining fully alert. I looked back only when I was waiting for Jean as she rummaged through some goods or other. Eye contact with the odd stallholder told me they knew exactly who we were. It was unsettling. The market consisted of about two hundred stalls. It was the biggest I'd seen. Jean was in her element; she loved shopping. I was wondering how long it would take before I got bored. Probably an hour at the most as there was no scenery. All the girls were wrapped up against the cold wind. Jean would see something, then go and rummage. I would stand in the aisle and wait. Not that I wasn't interested. I wasn't! It was just that she looked at so many things. I just didn't see the point of following her every inch of the way. If she wanted me to have a look at something she would come over, grab my arm and pull me to the stall, and she would whisper. This went on for about forty-five minutes. Then she saw something that really excited her. She looked over her shoulder, forgot herself and said, "Come over here Jack."

A typical-looking family man in his mid-forties. Grey hair and quite well dressed spun on his heel and glared. Spittle sprayed from his tight lips as he said, "Fucking Brits. Why don't you piss off home."

I caught Jean's eye and nodded towards the car. It wasn't so much him, we didn't know how others would react. It was the unknown that directed me. I can still remember to this day the venom he spat those words out with. The words were followed by a look of sorrow and remorse on his face. A bygone memory resurfacing in his mind. You couldn't help but feel sorry for him.

The car would have to be checked for suspect devices anytime it was left in a public place where access could be gained by terrorists. I opened the boot, took out a sheet of plastic, placed it on the ground and felt foolish. People watched and smiled as I checked. I wasn't sure which was the worst – being humiliated or blown up. There is a problem with checking your car in public. If anyone watching didn't know you were a member of the Security Forces before, they did now. The other option was to park your car in a police station if there was one nearby and deny the terrorists access. This raised a problem. The IRA positioned spotters outside police stations and army camps who noted car registrations. If they didn't know you were Security Forces before you entered the police station, they did after. For every plus on this planet, there's a minus.

4

HELLO CHRIS – AGAIN

The weather had improved as we rolled into summer. There was still a lot of rain, but it was much warmer. Jean's confidence and mine had improved enough for us to take up golf. We practised and practised until we'd perfected the Irish pronunciation of *fore* before venturing out. Neither of us had played before, but we had some great weekends learning. I spent more time in bunkers than Hitler did in the whole of the Second World War.

The golf course was occasionally out of bounds. This was because information trickled in about bombs being planted, or of a possible targeting of personnel on the course. But that was par for the course. Trevor from The Troop played golf and, when I mentioned that Jean and I were going for a round, he asked if he could come along. It was one of those glorious days that seemed to be made for golf. The sun was shining and a gentle breeze blew to keep us cool. We'd decided on an eight o'clock start to miss the rush. The three of us chattered away merrily as we made our way to the first tee. Jean and I were coming in with scores around the one hundred and twenty mark, which doesn't sound good. But, as we had started with scores of one hundred and thirty odd, there was a definite improvement. Trevor was a much more accomplished golfer. He spent a lot of time waiting for us to find lost balls, but it didn't seem to bother him. The Brigadier was out enjoying this beautiful morning. He was too far away to recognize, but you couldn't miss him with a wide, loose circle of six armed soldiers corralling him as he played.

Earlier I'd noticed an unusual pocket on Trevor's golf bag and it was while we were waiting for Jean to find another lost ball that I asked him about it. He smiled, leaned the bag towards me and said, "Have a look."

The pocket was on the inside of the bag and had a top cover press-studded over it. I popped the press-studs, flipped open the cover and found myself looking down the barrel of a HK53. Trevor was smiling when I looked up. He said, "Can't take any chances, can you?"

We came to a tee where a canal ran alongside. It reminded me of a round I'd had earlier with Fred Tech.

"You know Fred Tech?" I asked. "Well, he'd been pushing me for ages for a game because his wife had bought him a new one wood for his birthday and he was dying to try it out. One day we went out and every opportunity that cropped up he'd pull it out. 'The one wood,' I said before they could say anything." I pulled my one wood out of my bag to demonstrate his actions.

"He'd pull it out and stroke it," I said, stroking the club. "Then he'd drool over it. After the shot he'd tell me how good it was. Well, all of a sudden the heavens opened, and it poured," I told them lifting my arms to show how heavy it had been. "It was one of those cloudbursts that feels like somebody has poured a bucket of water over you and Fred hadn't any waterproofs. He just stood there. Pissed off. Soaked to the skin with a mega sad on. 'Get your one wood out and make this the drive of the day,' I told him, trying to cheer him up. He took his top off." I ran through the actions of taking my top off. "Then he threw it to the ground." I swung my arm down angrily to emphasize his mood. Then stood behind the tee as he had done. "He pictured the shot going down the fairway. Sheer concentration all the way. He took his time as he lined up. Looked down the fairway, adjusted slightly, then it was eye on the ball. The club was coming down fast. You could even see every ounce of his energy being transferred into the club head. He hit the ball clean as a whistle. Carried on through to the top of the swing, and that's when it happened," I said holding my club up. "He lost his grip. The club slipped out of his hands and sailed over those trees," I said, pointing. "And landed in the canal. He just stood there with his mouth wide open. Staring at the canal. Looking even more dejected. I tried not to laugh," I told them. "Managed to hold it for thirty seconds. Couldn't keep it in any longer. Then roared."

It had been a good morning. I finished with a round of one hundred and five. Managed to loose two balls, which wasn't unusual, and managed to find three, which wasn't unusual either.

Monday morning Roy was pointing to some hills on a map. Explaining a comms problem we were having.

"Londonderry is set in a valley with the River Foyle running through it," he said. "On one side of the river is the Catholic enclave, and on the other the Protestant. The problem we've got is on the Catholic side. There are dead spots in the radio coverage, and the problem's been going on for ages. This is really Paul YoS's job," he said looking up. "But you know how useless he is," he whispered. "Paul even got a consultant in because he couldn't sort it. The consultant recommended siting the antenna on a mast and gave a grid reference. I was really puzzled," he said, opening his arms in dismay. "I thought I'd tried all the masts, but I didn't recognize this one. When I checked the coordinates, the mast he'd recommended was on the other side of the border. So much for consultants. Well," he said, drawing out the word and smiling, "a new mast has been built and I thought if we went up tomorrow, took the techs with us, we could do the rigging and they could install the equipment. We could get the operators to do the coverage trials later and we could leave the old equipment in as a fall-back. Just in case the coverage trials are crap."

We set off early the next day. Roy was in the front car with Tony Bleep. Ray Tech and I were following. We crossed the Foyle into the Catholic side and the atmosphere was heavy. Pedestrians stared into cars, viewed the occupants with suspicion and, if they didn't recognize them, stared even more. It was unnerving. A look of belonging to the area had to be projected and it wasn't easy. Past the wall murals proclaiming Free Derry. Then past the police station and, boy, was it fortified. I hung onto the pistol grip of the MP5 which lay across my lap under a jacket, ready for any problems, grateful the only set of lights we went through was on green. We arrived at the mast, relieved, and un-loaded the stores. Roy and Tony wanted to rig the antenna. I had no objection. I'd been up enough masts since I'd arrived. Glad to sit this one out.

They climbed and began fixing the antenna while Ray and I stood at the bottom. On the way up we'd discussed organizing a barbecue and we bounced the idea around again.

"Everybody is so pissed off at the moment, I think it's a great idea," I said.

"Yeah, it would be good for morale. There are still people here I haven't met and I've been here twelve months," said Ray.

"I reckon £15 per head should give unlimited beer and food. What do you think, Ray?"

"Yeah that sounds fine. What we could do is meet tomorrow, work out a date and go round to see who's interested."

I stepped back and looked up to see how they were getting on and noticed one single black cloud drifting towards them.

"Nimbus approaching," I shouted up the mast.

"What the fuck's that?" asked Roy.

"It's a cloud formation that means rain somewhere. And, there is also a high lightning risk factor."

"That's the biggest load of bullshit I've heard for ages," he shouted back.

I was leaning on the mast as it approached and stepped away, just in case. Ray followed. CRACK! BOOM! Bright vivid lightning forked down and hit the mast, momentarily blinding me and leaving pinprick white spots in my vision. You could actually hear the lightning running down the mast to ground. It sounded like rust particles falling down vertical steel tubes. I looked up, expecting to see them hanging limply in their belts and wondering how I was going to get them down, but I was really suprised to see them running down. They jumped the last few feet to the ground and Ray and I roared. I'd never seen anything like it before. Their hair actually stood on end. Tony was seriously rattled and wouldn't go up again. I offered to finish the job, but Roy said no, he'd do it. He had to, really, especially after the comment he'd made, or he'd never have lived it down.

We ran into a checkpoint on the way back manned by green teams (soldiers in uniform). We were covert and wanted to remain that way, so stayed in the queue. I put my driving licence into the outstretched hand of the lance corporal and said nothing, just like every other driver, and watched his face, just like any other driver.

There was a moment's hesitation as he took in the contents.

"I'd like to look in the boot," he said.

He was an experienced soldier and was not going to blow our cover by giving an easy passage. I slipped the pistol from under my thigh, placed it under the seat and climbed out. To anyone watching he made a thorough search of the boot, but he saw nothing. He gave me my licence back, then waved to a soldier down the road.

The soldier down the road was bored shitless. His job was to walk to the middle of the road dragging a chain behind him, then back to the kerb dragging the same chain behind him. The chain was made up of steel spikes and was laid across the road to prevent anyone from leaving in a hurry. He must have done it a hundred times a day and walked miles. No wonder he was bored shitless.

Ray told me about a checkpoint he went through last year.

"It was a young lad who checked me," he said. "Probably on his first tour. 'Let this one through,' he'd shouted. 'He's one of ours.' I might as well have had security forces painted on the side," he laughed. "I changed the car the next day and it was shipped back."

I called in to see Ray the next morning. Rang the ops room to let them know where I was and put the kettle on. Ray arrived ten minutes later, beaming from ear to ear.

"Get your nookies last night?" I asked.

He didn't need to answer. His grin just got bigger.

Frank was copying blue movies, as usual, and came over with Stan and John Tech when they heard BBQ. They were all for it, so we choose a Saturday in four weeks' time, divided up the departments and went round canvassing.

Nick Chief, the new chief clerk, was first on my list. He was one of those skinny people with a fast metabolism. One of those that could eat and drink as much as they liked, but never put weight on. He seemed to have endless bouncy energy and was always chirpy. This was in spite of the fact his wife used to beat the shit out of him on a regular basis. He was all for the BBQ. On the way round I told everybody about Roy and the lightning so they could wind him up. Somebody came up with Flash Gordon. It stuck. Paul YoS and Jim FoS declined; we were all glad.

We met after lunch and compared lists. The response had been good, so Ray and I began listing the stores we'd need: tents with sides that could be rolled up or down, depending on the weather, boxes that could be filled with ice to keep the beer cold, refrigerators and a generator, cricket bat, volley ball, badminton rackets, tennis rackets, beach bowls and football, transport, radio comms, steel locker for weapons, cutlery, paper napkins and black bags for the rubbish. If we thought we might use it, we ordered it. We were going all out with this one. Everything was planned down to the last detail. Everything was done that same afternoon. Stores were ordered, transport booked and the unit warned that patrolled the beach. Ray said he'd place an order for the steaks, burgers and sausages at the local butchers on his way home and order loads of bread rolls.

A week later Ray and I were out again. The job was routine maintenance at a location situated near the border, but posed no problems. You can normally see the mast from a distance, as they are mostly situated on hilltops, but today was different. Low cloud shrouded the hills and we couldn't see a thing. Orienteering had been one of my sports in the past so I reached for the map, relishing the opportunity of guiding Ray straight onto the mast. Visibility dropped to about thirty yards as we climbed the hill, but I still felt confident, rapping off lefts and rights.

"We should have been there half an hour ago," I told Ray.

"What does that mean?" he asked.

"We're fucking lost," I said.

"There's a signpost over there," said Ray pointing. We drove over, then I looked on the map for Mill Town. Not wanting to panic him. I quietly said, "It would be a good idea if we turned round."

"Do you know where we are?" he asked.

"Sure. I'm absolutely positive. We're in Southern Ireland."

"In that case let's get the hell out'a here," he said.

The job wasn't urgent. Routine maintenance that could be done another day. So not wanting to chance another cock-up, we binned the job and headed back.

The following day Brian was the first person I saw at work. He inclined his head, inviting me over.

"I see John Tech got pinged last night. At Woodbourne," he said.

"Is he all right?"

"Yeah. The shots came from a block of flats on the other side of the road. But they missed."

John had been on a night climb. It was too risky to climb during the day at Woodbourne. I thought about going to see him, but he would probably have got his head down. He'd be in the bar tonight. He never missed a Friday session. I'd catch him then.

Brian and I had been on the lookout for office space.

"I've found an office big enough for two. Do you want to share?" he asked.

"Can we have a look now?"

"Sure, it's just opposite the front door. Come on."

It was just right. Large enough for two and not inside the main block. We'd need a lot more than the two desks and one table that were there. So Brian and I decided a redistribution of office supplies was required. It turned out to be a hilarious morning, as one of us would keep somebody talking while the other one nicked something. We begged, stole and long-term borrowed practically everything that morning. People wised up in the afternoon and told us to piss off if we so much as popped our heads round their door.

I was putting in something like sixty or seventy hours a week and the workload was still increasing. Paul YoS had applied for an extra man for me and he came into my new office to tell me Chris was arriving on Monday and would be with me for six months.

Chris was about twenty-three. He looked sixteen. He had ginger hair. He had white skin covered in freckles and he had a long, gangly, thin six-foot frame of a body. I'd met him in Belize, but had doubts as to whether he would cope with this job. I remembered him telling me about the problems that being in Belize created for him, when it came to watching his favorite soap, *Home and Away*. He'd said his girlfriend used to record every episode for him for when he got home. But that wasn't the end.

"There was a problem," he'd told me. "When I go back, I can't watch the ones being televised, or I'd go out of sequence. What I have to do is tape the ones being televised and slot them in at the end. I have to watch four hours of *Home and Away* every day," he'd complained, smilingly. "It was the only way I could catch up." Mind-bending.

The day rolled on until that special time came. Bar time. Our crowd had assembled in a corner of the bar and we were waiting for John. A huge cheer erupted as he came through the door and we all waved a can of beer at him. He came over with that jaunty walk of his, holding his arm out for the first beer. The lads couldn't wait and urged him, "What happened last night?"

He took a few mouthfuls, settled in, relaxed and hung it out.

"I'd been up the mast for a couple of hours, minding my own business and quietly working away," he said as he took another sip. "It was about half two," he continued in a whisper, "when it happened."

We were having difficulty in hearing, and we had to lean forward.

"*Crack*," he shouted.

We all jumped back and burst out laughing from the shock. He smiled after the wind up, looked us all in the eye and carried on.

"I've never been shot at before, but I knew instantly what it was," he said in a normal voice. "I actually felt the wind of it as it passed my head," he said, moving his left hand over his head. "Boy, did I move. I've never moved so fast in my whole life." He paused as he mentally relived it. We waited, not wanting to disturb him. He seemed suddenly to remember where he was. He looked up, and continued: "I don't remember unclipping my belt. I just remember being halfway down. Then two more rounds passed," he said, moving his hand past his head again, twice. "Next thing I know I'm on the ground." His eyes were sparkling, his movements over-exaggerated and he was talking ten to the dozen. Adrenalin was still pumping round his system. It would be a while before he could wind down.

Friday night had kicked off. The talk and the hoots of laughter got louder as the evening wore on.

"Anybody coming down the strip?" shouted John.

"We'll join you later," said most.

The Strip is a number of bars and squadron clubs which are congregated together on the same road in camp. Ray, John and I set off. We passed a girl on the way down. I couldn't believe what Ray did when we drew level. He picked up a twig, threw it across the front of her and said, "Fetch."

She went absolutely ballistic and was all ready to get stuck into him. I stepped in and lied, told her he'd been shot at today and was not thinking straight. Ray and John walked on ahead, giggling. Left me to it, the bastards. Consoling her took some time and, still fuming, she grudgingly let it go.

I found them in Three Nine Brigade's bar. They were by the door taking the mickey out of Scouse Wheels who'd got his leg in plaster. He said he'd been playing football that afternoon and received a dirty tackle.

"No driving for a while," he said. "But I'm looking forward to just sitting in that office for six weeks."

"Ah, so that's why you did it. So you could have a rest," said John.

Scouse got up-tight. He didn't like being called lazy, but before he could say anything we went to the bar. The rest of the lads trickled in and joined us. We bunched together, forming a large circle at the bar, dominating the area with noise and jostle. Everybody gave us space.

It was about ten o' clock when I knew I'd had enough. I'd reached the double vision stage where the only way I could focus on anything was by closing one eye.

"Do you want a beer?" asked Ray.

I looked at him. He looked at me, smiled, and began winking at me.

"I've had enough Ray. I'm going home."

"Me too."

"Before we go lets nick Scouse's crutches," I said.

Ray and John's eyes took on a mischievous look and I knew they were for it.

"Take him a pint over and stand between him and his crutches. While you're talking to him I'll nick his crutches. Then we can meet in the bogs. Break them into pieces and throw them at him on the way out," I suggested.

Scouse was over the moon with another free beer. The lads were looking after him tonight and he merrily chatted away, completely unaware.

We met in the bogs, laughing and joking as we broke them. We were on such a high that uncontrollable laughter kept bubbling up inside of us. The laughter was practically beyond control. It took us all our time to keep it in as we stood in front of Scouse. I reached for the door, opened it and said, "See you Scouse."

He raised his hands for protection as his crutch pieces sailed towards him. We rushed out of the door.

"Bastards," he shouted after us.

We stood outside acting like devilish schoolboys. We were roaring with laughter and unable to control it. People passing gave us a wide berth, sensing we didn't give a fuck in our drunken state. We didn't.

I set off home and, boy, was the beer beginning to hit. The further I went the more I swayed. By the time I reached the football pitches I was staggering. The pitches had been cut out of a slope and levelled off, giving them two steep sides. I one eye focused and looked at one of the steep sides. It was enormous and seemed to have grown since the last time I saw them. Good job I'd done that mountaineering course I thought, and chuckled. I just couldn't stop chuckling. Chuckling had taken hold of me and I was so happy. I ran a three-miler twice a week and was reasonably fit, but climbing this slope seemed so incredibly hard. I made a mental note to work out more. Half-way up I caught my toe on a tuft of grass.

It made me stagger slightly. Only a little bit, but enough to put me off balance. I rolled to the bottom and lay there, chuckling. I was totally aware of what I had to do, but incapable of doing it. I lay there working out my next move: how to climb Everest. If I walked back a few paces then I could take a run at it!

The chuckling had to subside first though. I tried to suppress it, but only made it worse. Take your mind off it. Look at the sky.

Which one's Pluto? Which one's Saturn? Okay. Ready. I drew in deep breaths, stood up, counted ten paces back. Total concentration. One eye closed for focus. Kneel down – feet on blocks. There was an imaginary man standing at the side, holding a starting pistol at arms length. Bang! I was off.

I hurtled toward the slope and zoomed up it. The wind whistled around my head as it met me at the top. I felt I was doing a hundred miles an hour. I couldn't work out why I was suddenly running sideways, and downward when I was supposed to be running up. My body was moving forward faster than my legs. I tried running faster to bring my legs back in line with my body, but it was no use. I knew exactly what was going to happen, but couldn't do a damn thing about it. I landed face down. I skidded to the bottom, and finished up exactly where I'd started. This was incredibly funny.

I decided to have a fag and think about it. Anybody passing would have thought I was a complete and utter nut lying in the damp grass, looking up at the stars, laughing and having a fag. I thought about dozing off and spending the night there. It seemed the easy way out, but Jean would have reported me missing and a search would have been organized. It had to be home.

Fag finished. Decision made. I crawled up the slope. Then crawled twenty yards along the pitch, just to be sure that I didn't stagger backwards and fall down the slope again. I couldn't be that pissed if I was making these sorts of calculations and decisions, I thought. I weaved across the pitch and headed for home, covering twice the distance I needed. I reached a road and stopped to regain my breath and get my bearings. I think I'm going the wrong way, I told myself.

I can still remember the sound of the electric window opening.

I can still remember the colour of the car, dark blue. To this day, I still don't know who the voice belonged to.

"Are you alright Jack?"

I stared through one eye and tried to focus, but it was becoming increasingly difficult as my head was now swaying from side to side and backwards and forwards like a week-old baby.

"Where are you going?" asked Mr Anonymous.

I tried three times to say home, but I was having problems with my H's. I knew exactly what I wanted to say. My brain was clear. It was just my tongue. I'd lost control of it.

"Are you going home?" he asked.

I was totally elated that he had got that word out for me and I moved my head backwards and forwards like one of those dogs that car owners put in their back window. I opened the door, slid my body on to the front passenger seat and grinned one of those stupid grins that can only be produced when you are totally incapable. My shoulders sagged and my body flopped forward. My head banged on the dash so I leaned back. The headrest prevented a serious case of backlash injury. I directed the driver by grunting and giving left and right hand signals. I wound down the window, hoping it would sober me up. It didn't. Several times on that short journey I fell against the Good Samaritan and each time he pushed me back into the upright position and never once complained. To this day I don't know whether he was following my directions (which I doubt) or he knew where I lived.

I looked down the path to the front of the house and the path was a thousand miles long. I needed guts and determination for this next great adventure in my life so I gulped, searched for and finally found the car door handle. I knew I had to be vertical to get out, but I couldn't get there. Major decision time again I told myself. My brain clicked and whirred until the solution fell into place. The solution was so simple I wondered why I had taken so long to come up with it. My knees painfully hit the tarmac pavement two seconds after my feet. My hands followed closely after.

I knew where I was. My brain was okay. What had happened to my body? The front door to the house opened and there stood

Jean, laughing. I heard the car pull away and I remember Jean waving to the driver.

"You'll have to go round to the back door," she said. "You're covered in mud."

It seemed to take for ever to crawl round the back. Then it was a repeat of two minutes ago. Jean was stood at the door, laughing. She wouldn't let me in.

"Too much mud on you. Undress here while I run the bath," she said, before disappearing. I'd got into the standing position, somehow, and I now stood with my back against the wall. I needed to use my hands to undress but the palms were in pain. I turned them upward to see what was the matter and looked at them. I realized what the problem was so I rubbed them together. Black and white chippings of tarmac fell off my palms and cascaded around my feet. I checked my hands for the all clear and noticed the tiny sharp indentation that each pellet of gravel had left. I rubbed my hands up and down my legs to try and erase the indentations, then began to undress. I was stood there, shivering in my shreddies when the door opened again. Boy, did I need help. I bounced off every wall and tripped over every stair on the way to the bathroom, and that was with Jean steering me. The bath felt luxurious. I lay there letting the heat seep into my body, not ever wanting to move again. Jean came back up when she heard me snoring, shook me, dried me, helped me to bed.

We went to the mess the following night and sat with Robbie Wheels, Brad, the new FoS who ran the tech workshops, and his wife Wendy.

"Where was your last posting Brad?" I asked.

"I was with the marines in Plymouth," he said with a superior look on his face.

"Our son's serving with two nine Commando," I told him. "Did you have any contact with them?"

"No. Different location," he told me.

John Tech was one of his lads, and after the shooting Brad had come up with a cunning plan to get off a mast fast. It was really new and interesting! Abseiling.

"I want to arrange a demo for fast descents off masts," he said.

"Would you be interested? I'll do the talking. All you have to do, is abseil off the top."

"OK, I'll give it a go," I said.

Robbie was on form that night. He was firing non-stop jokes and generally embarrassing everybody. We were all piling in with retorts, and it was turning out to be one of those nights. Brad prided himself on his drinking capabilities, but seemed to be more sloshed than us.

"Where's your drinking head tonight?" I asked him.

"Had a few this afternoon," he said, "and they're catching up."

"Well, you'd better stay sober for the next ten minutes," I told him. "It's your round. Come on, I'll give you a lift."

He had that 'I'm the greatest' walk about him. His imaginary green lid was on his head. This is a state which super-fit soldiers (Marines, Paras, etc) reach when they are pissed, or not pissed, whatever the case might be. They think the rest of the population can see their invisible beret. They also think they're Rambos, invincible, and can take on the world.

We stood at the bar, watching snooker in the next room through a serving hatch, waiting to be served. Brad started sniffing, twitching his nose. Just little sniffs to begin with, then bigger and deeper ones. I sniffed too, wondering if he'd dropped his guts. He looked down. I followed. Right beneath his nose was an ashtray. Brad was a strict non-smoker. Smoking in his office was a definite no no. If you stood near him smoking, he'd let you know.

"Fucking smokers," he yelled, picking up the ashtray and launching it through the hatch. The ashtray bounced right in front of a player's cue, just as he was about to shoot. Dog ends and ash flew into the air. Then they settled on the table and the player's arm. Chatter ceased. A hush descended around the bar and some of the men took one step forward. A dodgy situation.

"I'll take care of it," I said, holding my arm out with my hand vertical. The people who had taken one step forward stopped, watched. I grabbed Brad's arm and dragged him back to our table. Wendy looked up when we got back. She knew something was wrong.

"Look after him Wendy. He's stepping out of line," I told her.

She was used to it and gave him a withering look. He took the look on board and sat down, quiet as a church mouse. He may be tough, but Wendy was boss. The evening turned out to be a cracker, Brad's little incident only adding to the excitement.

I was first in on Monday morning and sat at my new desk in my new office, having a cuppa and a fag when Brian walked in. I watched him for the first time as he off-loaded a Browning from a shoulder holster. Small pistol from the back of his waistband and, to top it all, an even smaller two-shot pistol from a holster, fastened to his ankle.

"Just de-tooling," he said, smiling, putting the weapons in the top drawer of his filing cabinet. They would be safe there. We always locked the office when we were out and most of the time when we were in.

At about eleven someone tried the door. It was locked. I looked at Brian, doing his crossword. He looked up, shook his head. We stayed quiet.

"Chris is here Jack," shouted Paul YoS.

I looked at Brian, lifted my hands, palms up, shrugged my shoulders and opened the door. Chris stood there with a beaming smile on his face, hand outstretched. Paul followed him in and hovered in the background. We ignored Paul. He got the message and left.

"I've booked in and I'm free to start work right away," said Chris.

"Okay, let's get our priorities right," I replied. "Go and get yourself a coffee, and nick a chair while you're at it. Then I'll outline the job." He disappeared through the door and Brian started laughing.

"Who the fuck's that? Not the rigger that's come to help you?" he asked. Chris came back and sat down.

"Right. First thing on the agenda is an abseil demo in a couple of days," I said to him. Then I went on to outline the type of work we'd be doing.

"Mostly rigging," I told him, "with intercoms, telephone repairs and installations thrown in." I painted a picture of the Unit. Told

him about the weapons, vehicles and locations we'd be visiting –
and the BBQ.

Wednesday came and we loaded the abseil gear for the demo
into the van, then drove to a tower at the side of the football
pitches. The tower was next to the slope I'd crawled up and it
seemed so small and insignificant now.

"We won't be able to do the demo on this mast. The wind's too
strong," I told Brad.

"Let's try the sixty footer at the back of tech workshops. It's
sheltered there."

"Let's give it a go before everybody arrives," Brad said.

I didn't see the point, but complied. I fed the rope down from
the top of the tower and the wind caught it, blew it through the
tower and around girders.

"Forget it Jack," he shouted. "We'll use the one at tech workshops."

Typical technician, I thought. No common sense. It was all right
for him. I had to scramble all over the tower and untangle the rope.

"Due to high winds the demo will now take place behind tech
workshops," Brad told the waiting throng. We stood, waiting for
Brad to begin, again!

"It will take time to set up," he began. "But there are benefits
in a fast descent." He talked them through the set-up procedure
while I carried it out. I rested at the top, looked down and waited.
Brad stepped away from the mast. He looked up and shouted,
"Okay." They all looked up, and waited. I wanted to make it look
as professional as possible and was hoping to jump off and reach the
ground in two leaps. It was a disaster and turned out to be the most
painful abseil I'd ever done. Going down a wall which has a flat
smooth surface or coming off an overhang into an open space is
fine. The problem here was that the mast was wider at the bottom
than top, and I had to continually push myself away. This may
sound easy, but, as the cross-sectional supporting struts of the tower
were thin, I kept missing them.

I'd started off with a large leap, then swung in to push myself
off. I missed the strut and grazed my shins and knocked my knees
as my legs went inside the mast. The leaps got smaller the more

69

pain I received. Ten feet from the bottom I lowered myself by stepping from strut to strut. Brad tried to cover by saying how you must slow down as you neared the bottom.

PPP&P means PPP (Piss Poor Planning and Preparation means Piss Poor Performance) were my only thoughts as I hit the ground, in tears. It would be four days before I could walk properly.

5

THE BBQ

This week was going to be busy. I had to be at the airport on Wednesday to collect our youngest daughter Jane who was home for half term. I was preparing for the BBQ on Saturday, plus there was a fault at Woodbourne that needed sorting. I didn't want the Woodbourne job spilling into the weekend, so I made arrangements for Tuesday night.

A new policy had come into force. It stated that rigging anywhere had to be carried out at night. It would have been a night climb at Woodbourne anyway. It was quickly followed by another directive stating the only way in and out of Woodbourne was by armoured pig.

I guided Chris through the records, took the necessary details for Woodbourne, then headed for the riggers' shack. Chris was new to rigging, so I went through the various cables, antennae, connectors and stores. Then I talked him through making up a feeder cable and attaching an antenna. There was a loading list pinned to the back of the door.

"We go through this every time we load," I told him. I threw a bunch of keys to him. "It's the red Ford Transit on the square. Check it out and bring it over, will you?"

I watched through the window as he checked the water, oil, battery and windscreen washer. On to the lights, indicators and finally tyre pressures, including the spare. I was impressed. The journey to Woodbourne wasn't far, but we were reducing the odds. Chris drove the van over and we started loading.

"Van Okay?" I asked.

"Yeah, but the fuel tank's half empty."

"What are you going to do about it?"

"As soon as we've finished loading, I'll go to the petrol point," he replied.

"Once you've tanked up call it a day," I told him.

We met at ten the next morning and ran through the weapons. He wanted more practice, so I left him to it. Later, I outlined the night's events.

"We'll meet in control at half nine and start booking out. Probably arrive in Woodbourne about half ten. We'll leave the climb until two in the morning for two reasons," I said. "It's a lovely summer's night and it will probably be at its darkest then, and most people will have got their heads down by that time. The antenna we're checking is still being used, but the transmission is crackly," I said.

We met at half nine and started to book out. Support weapons, full magazines and smoke grenades went into a holdall. Brownings with full mags were tucked into our belts. Details were entered into the book. We climbed into the van and fidgeted until everything was just right and within easy reach. We did a radio check and we were off.

The nearer we got, the quieter it got. Not a car in sight as we drove down the road with the fortified walls of the station on our right. There were no lights for obvious reasons, so I slowed and scanned, searching for the gate. We came to a corner, turned right and drove up a side street. We came across a gate, pulled up in front and sat waiting. The gate looked dormant, unused and lifeless, and Chris and I began to wonder whether we were at the right one. Five minutes later we decided to move. This was because two men had appeared and were walking towards us, the only moving things we'd seen in the last half-mile. HKs came out of hiding and lay across our laps as I reversed and headed for the main road. We cruised back in the direction we'd come from, fully alert. If we didn't spot it this time we were going back. I wasn't going to ask for directions around here. We saw it this time, deep in the shadows of the trees in full foliage, buried against prying eyes. We pulled up

72

and waited. A loud clunk was followed by a whirring noise. One half of the steel gate drew back on its hydraulic piston. They'd been warned of our arrival so we drove in, but were stopped from entering camp by another steel gate. The first gate slammed shut behind us and the sound increased momentarily as it bounced off the coffin walls and dived in and out of the deep shadows within before dying out and leaving a deathly silence. The moonlight reflecting off the tops of the steel walls gave a horror-film feel to the situation. We were startled by a voice from nowhere,

"IDs?" asked the voice.

A rash of goose pimples burst over my body as I turned to my right and saw a half-man half-shadow three feet away. There was no real shape to this being. He had not one inch of reflective surface on his body and his hot breath steamed vertically, giving him a wraith-like appearance. He held out his left arm to receive identification from us while cuddling his rifle with his right. The rifle seemed to be attached to his body, as though he had grown an extra limb. He returned our IDs, stepped back into the shadows and once again disappeared. I heard him whisper into his radio and the inner gate opened, breaking the silence.

First stop was the ops room to book in and tell them what we were doing. One of the soldiers overheard. "You wouldn't get me up that tower for love nor money," he said. It was a well-used sentence, repeated on many an occasion.

"Don't walk across the square," said the ops room officer. "It's exposed and the inhabitants of the flats across the road like to send the odd round in." We complied.

We parked below the mast, climbed out of the van and looked up. The mast was one hundred feet tall, situated near the wall and definitely overloaded. By how much, I wondered? It was quarter past eleven. Too light to climb, so we relaxed. We dug out the flask and listened to the radio, talking and passing time.

"Did I tell you about the coolest operator Brian had ever known?" I asked Chris.

"No."

"Well the operator," I began, "had been on surveillance in one of the streets around here. Two men approached him from behind and split when they reached him. One walked to the passenger door and the other to the driver's door." There was a lot of time between now and the climb so I sipped my coffee, then carried on.

"The one at the driver's door tapped on the window with a Browning, and asked him to open the passenger door." I sipped more coffee. Three hours is a lot of time to kill. "Brian said the operator looked at the Browning."

"As you do," said Chris.

"Yeah, as you do," I said. "Well, the operator noticed the Browning was on half cock."

"As you do," Chris said again.

"Is there any chance of me finishing this tonight?" I asked.

"Well, it's got to last three hours because we can't climb until two," he replied.

It was going to be one of those nights. I gave up. Ten minutes later Chris said, "Okay, he'd noticed it was on half cock."

I wasn't going to be rushed into it so I took my time before carrying on. Ten minutes later I was ready.

"Right. Well, this meant he would have to fully cock the weapon before he could fire it. The one at the passenger door was the greatest threat, as the operator didn't know if he was carrying. It was do or die really. So the operator whips his pistol from under his thigh, releases the safety and takes out the one at the passenger door, then the one at the driver's door. Brian said the operator didn't hang around and when the security forces arrived; the only sign that the terrorists had been there was a pool of blood on the floor."

"Cool Hand Luke," said Chris.

"Is there any chance I might get any sense out of you tonight?" I asked again.

"Half one," I said, looking at my watch. "Come on. We can start testing."

There were no operations on tonight. We'd checked. The only people using this transmitter were Chris and I. I contacted our ops room on an alternative channel and told them we were starting on the faulty transmitter. I disconnected the feeder cable from the transmitter equipment, inserted a through line test meter and took

74

the reading. The meter would prove whether it was the antenna or the equipment that was faulty. It was the antenna.

"What next?" asked Chris.

"It's up the mast and search for the antenna. You start at the top, and I'll start at the bottom. Whoever finds it opens the joint and lets it hang to dry if there's water in it. Then we'll climb down and wait. We'll give it half an hour. Then one of us can go back up and re-connect while the other does the testing. If the test proves okay, we can seal the cable and go home."

It was still very light, but it was not going to get any darker.

"Belts on. Lets go," I said.

I watched Chris as he climbed. It was a steady, easy climb and he was happy with the heights. All my earlier fears were disappearing and the old adage about never judge a book by its cover came to mind. He climbed down from the top and I climbed up from the bottom. We met in the middle, talked in whispers, not wanting our voices to carry on the moist night air.

"Did you find it?" he asked.

"No. Did you?"

"There was one without a number on; it must be that one," said Chris.

"I found one without a number as well," I told him.

"What are we going to do?"

"Check them all again. I'll check the top half this time. You check the bottom. If we don't find it we'll meet on the ground."

I moved onto another face of the mast so I wouldn't have to scramble over Chris and made my way up, checking numbers. We met on the ground.

"What are we going to do now?" he asked.

"We'll have to trace the cable from the equipment then up the mast. We could put a new antenna up and forget the old one," I said, "but the mast is so overloaded I don't want to take that chance."

There were twelve antennae on the mast and their feeder cables were zip-tied down the same leg. Each feeder would have been zipped as it was installed. We could finish up cutting hundreds of zips if ours was one of the first rigged.

75

"Leave three zips intact near each antenna," I told Chris, "so the weight of the cable doesn't pull the joint apart."

We started at the transmitter, traced the feeder to the mast and climbed, leap frogging each other whilst cutting the zips.

THUMP! A high-velocity round hit a wall in camp. We shifted off that mast.

"What now?" asked Chris.

Dawn was breaking. There was a gunman. Only one choice really. We re-connected the feeder cable to the equipment. Then we loaded and told control we were leaving.

We slept until lunchtime. Met at one, and arranged to meet an armoured pig at Mushgrave Camp at twenty two hundred Thursday. Then I let control know. Chris disappeared to sort some admin problems. I went to see Ray Tech about the BBQ.

"All the stores have arrived. I'll load them into the riggers' van on Friday, and we can meet at nine on Saturday. It'll give us time to set everything up before the main party arrives," said Ray.

"Chris and Tony Bleep said they'd give us a lift," I told Ray.

"I know," said Ray. "It'll be nice to have some help."

"Only one slight hitch," I told him.

"What's that?"

"The re-visit to Woodbourne. If we can get that out of the way there won't be any problems."

I showed my ID at the airport.

"Can I get in without going through the metal detectors," I asked the security guard.

"Are you carryin'?"

I nodded.

"The only way in is to hand your weapon over at the security desk. Then collect it on the way out," he said.

It meant drawing attention. I decided to wait. Jane would see me if she looked round.

Jane started to search as soon as she entered the arrivals lounge. She saw me and waved, smiled then joined the others. She'd been prewarned not to shout or talk too loud. Suitcase in hand, she headed for customs. I smiled inwardly, thinking about its contents. Ralph would be there. Ralph was a moth-eaten teddy with a scarf around his neck and he went everywhere that Jane went. He had probably flown more miles than most people had. She came through and we hugged and whispered, then made our way to the car. She waited patiently while I carried out the suspect device checks. Then it was climb aboard and non-stop chatter all the way. We were still in the car when the front door of the house opened and Jean came out with outstretched arms. They hugged and disappeared inside chattering and laughing. I grabbed the cases and followed. It was good to see her.

We were playing pool in the NAAFI at Mushgrave Camp when a corporal came in and asked if we were the party for Woodbourne. Chris picked up the holdall with the weapons in. It strained at the stitching and drew the corporal's eyes. He seemed entranced by it and just stared.

"Can you pull over to the car park so we can load some equipment?" I asked.

He looked up dazed. Finally worked out the answer and said, "Sure."

Their high-pitched whine sounded like living animals in pain as the pigs made their way over. The noise bounced off the walls of the low compact buildings. It met us, then left us. It reverberated down alleys and returned many times over. We were surrounded by pigs. Their screaming echoes attacked us from all directions. They cast out all other sound and gave an unreal not-of-this-world feeling.

I had never travelled in a pig before and it wasn't pleasant. The noise level was horrendous and the only way to communicate was by shouting. Couple the noise level with the confined space, the stench of sweaty bodies, the acidic smell of urine, the taste of fuel and we were only too glad to get out at Woodbourne. They dropped us off as close to the mast as they could. Then they helped us hump the kit over and left. "We're in luck tonight," I said, looking at the overcast sky. "It should be dark enough to climb by twelve. Then we'll carry on where we left off and trace the feeder. If there's water in the joint we let it dry. If there's no water in the joint we'll replace the old antenna and feeder," I told Chris.

At twelve we stood at the bottom of the mast and looked up.

"You know how we always change the route on the second visit," I said.

"Yeah," said Chris.

"Well, tonight we'll climb up the other leg."

I didn't think it was that funny, but Chris fell about laughing, and I had to wait for him to calm down. We traced the feeder up the mast and opened the joint – it was dry. Chris gave me a pissed-off look.

"What next?" he asked.

"You recover the old antenna while I go down for the new one," I told him.

"Below," Chris whispered in a sort of shout through funnelled hands so that his voice would only travel down. I looked up, saw him holding the antenna at arm's length and moved. Compacted cinders around the base of the mast meant that the antenna didn't bounce when it hit the ground. It just crunched and folded. I attached the new one to my belt and made my way up.

THUMP! They were at it again. The round had hit a building some distance away. It could be like this every night. Chris had a make-your-mind-up-quick look about him.

"Carry on," I whispered, handing him the antenna. I waited until it was loosely clamped, then started to descend, zipping the new and existing feeders to the leg.

THUMP! THUMP! Two more rounds thudded into a wall somewhere. Closer this time. It was difficult to pinpoint their exact impact points as the thump bounced off the buildings and came at us from several directions at the same time, but definitely closer. I looked up. Chris had closed down, concentrating totally on the job. At fifty feet I checked him again. He'd finished and was on his way down on the other side of the mast at a steady but urgent pace. We leap-frogged each other, zipping the feeder cable to the mast leg. We'd stop, hook one leg over a strut, do a couple of zips and move on.

THUMP! Fuck, we'd been spotted. The round fell short and hit the wall just below us.

"*Down*," I shouted. It just came out, but didn't need to be said. We galloped off that mast and I lost a few seconds of my life here.

I still don't remember the bit between "*down*" and being on the ground. We roared, calmed, then the shakes came.

"Let's have a coffee," I said to Chris. It's the last thing I should have asked for.

His hand was shaking. My hand was shaking, and between us we managed to spill more than we drank. I kept missing my mouth with my fag and we gibbered incoherently. We finally reached a point where we could understand what the other was saying.

"I don't want to come back again," I told Chris.

"What's the score then?"

"We'll climb to just below the top of the wall, zip the cables to the ground and leave the remainder for next rigger who comes along."

"Sounds fine by me," he agreed.

We finished, packed up and made our way to the ops room.

"Any chance of a pig out?" I asked the orderly officer.

The four of us were all geared up when we met on Saturday morning. We had everything we needed for a brilliant day and the last ingredient, the weather, had been forecast as hot and sunny. Chris and I jumped into the riggers' van and set off for the location, while John Bleep and Ray Tech went to pick up the meat, bread rolls, salad and ice. Chris and I had unloaded the equipment and were laying out the tent frame when John and Ray arrived. Ray was a bit tense.

"We'll have to get this food in the fridge straight away," he said, worried it was going to go off.

"The fridge is going to be working overtime if we leave it in the open. How about putting a tent up first, then bunging the fridge inside the tent to give it some shade?" I suggested. Everybody nodded consent, but Ray was still worried.

"Let's start the genny and put the meat in the fridge before we erect the tent," he persisted. The peace and calm were shattered when the genny roared into life. Seagulls that had been stood nearby having a nosey rose into the air and dumped all around us. We covered our heads, glad they weren't laser-guided. We put the meat into the fridge and moved onto the tent. It was one of those easy to erect tents with an aluminum frame that slotted together.

Step one was put the roof sections together. Step two was raise the roof and slot it on to half a leg. Step three was stretch the canvas over the half-erect frame, then position ourselves at each corner with the bottom half of a leg in one hand. They looked at me, waiting for something,

"Up," I said. We inserted the bottom half of the legs, rolled down and tied off the two sides facing west and south to provide shade, then drove a couple of spikes into the beach and tensioned off guys, just in case a breeze picked up. The genny was really getting on my nerves. I felt that if we had to sit with that in the background it would ruin the day.

"Doesn't the genny bother anybody?" I asked.

"Yeah," they chorused.

"We'll have to move it," I said.

"We've got a long mains cable," Ray said. "Why don't we stick it on the other side of the dunes?"

The genny was a meaty bit of kit and it took the four of us to hump it. Ray and John ran out the cable while Chris and I moved the fridge into the shade.

"How's that?" asked John from the top of a dune.

All we could hear was a low hum.

"It's fine. Do you think we should bury the cable?" I queried.

They moaned, picked up the shovels and dug. Put up the volley-ball court. Open the collapsible chairs and scatter them randomly around the tent. Put up the tables. Sort out the cutlery and napkins. Throw the ice and the beer into the boxes. Put the wine in the fridge and park up the van. The tasks seemed to go on for ever. Then all of a sudden we were looking around for the next one. It was ready.

They leapt off the bus yahoo-ing. Ripping off their shirts and asking where is it, while miming holding a can.

"In the tent," said Chris, moving out of the way of the stampede.

"Just look at them, they're like a bunch of kids. You'd have thought it was their first beer for a hundred years," said one of the wives.

They opened the boxes, splashed iced water over each other, laughed and shouted, savoured freedom, which is rare over there.

Clamping the pole to the top of Brutus.

The road to Brutus.

Tank Park.

Armoured Personnel Carriers.

Local Population.

The one and only hotel.

Posing in a downed Argentine Plane.

Posing (again) with a civvie contractor under Whale Bone Arch.

Large buildings from right to left – Officers Mess – Sergeants Mess – Other Ranks Mess.

One of the 'local' bars.

The top of Green Mountain.

A narrow path through a lava flow close by was named Snowman Pass.

Belizean Croc.

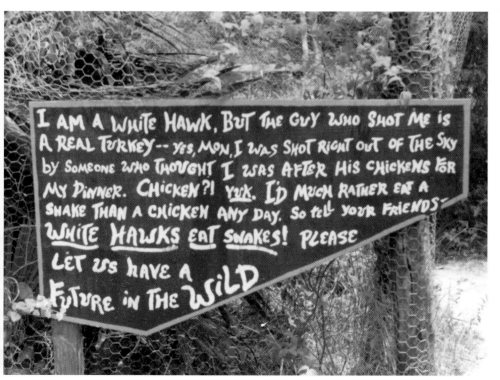

Sign next to an injured White Hawk.

Instead of having lunch, we could draw our rations, hire a water taxi and BBQ on one of the many small sandy islands.

Enjoying a cool beer in a warm sea

"Over here with your support weapons," I shouted while standing next to the metal locker. The beach was well patrolled; they still had their pistols.

Some people waded in the sea. Some played badminton, while some played tennis or beach bowls. Some sat around chatting, eating and sipping. It was turning into a great day.

"Anyone for volleyball?" shouted one of the lads.

There were enough for five on one side and six on the other. The game was slow to begin with, but improved the more we played. Rallies lasted longer and the whole game became more exciting. People even drifted over to watch, cheering or booing, depending on who they supported. Brummie Tech, a late arrival who'd obviously not had breakfast, made himself a triple burger, grabbed a beer and came over.

"Put the burger down Brum, we're one short," I told him.

Brum took an enormous bite from his burger and filled his mouth. Then he placed the burger and beer next to a net pole. He walked towards us, wiping his greasy fingers on his tee shirt and smiling at the girls.

"Ugh!" said the girls, pulling faces.

"Which is my position?" asked Brum through a gobful of burger. The girls ugh'ed again.

The next rally was a cracker. People were doing acrobatic dives to hit the ball, crashing into each other in their frantic efforts to keep it going, yelling at each other that the ball was theirs or mine. It didn't matter what you said, it was ignored. Off the court people were shouting and screaming. It was so noisy, exciting and funny that you couldn't help but get carried away. I set Brad up for a spike. He took it beautifully, driving it down towards the ground. The problem was Jean's head was in the way. It bounced off her and disappeared behind the dunes. We were in hysterics as Jean ducked under the net. She strode over to Brad and started to beat the shit out of him. We yelled and drove her on.

"Hit him harder. Kick him in the nuts," the nice girls shouted.

Brad couldn't take any more and ran off while Brum Tech went for the ball. I looked down and some dollops of horse shit caught my eye. The horse shit had dried into flat round cakes and looked remarkably like burgers. I tested a couple for density and solidity, chose the best and slipped it in Brum's burger. The ball appeared before Brum did. It sailed over the dunes and landed in the middle of us. Play resumed.

"Count me out for a minute, I'm hungry," said Brum when he got back.

We played at a slow pace. We watched and tried not to give anything away, all eyes were on Brum. The glaring sun marred his vision as he took a bite. He chewed, and watched the game. What game? A couple of us fell on our backs, laughing as his face contorted. He pulled the burger away and looked at it and the penny dropped. He scanned the court looking for the culprit. Never trust the girls.

"It was Jack," they yelled and pointed.

I was off down the beach with Brummie following, holding his beer. I could have run for miles, but what was the point? He would exact his retribution sooner or later, so I fell and lay there, waiting for my punishment. He started at my head and worked his way down, pouring his beer as he went along. He still had half a can left when he reached my balls, they were soaked.

I went over to the BBQ. I was too tired to play any more, so I grilled a steak. The others were in the same mood and followed. We talked, ate and drank. Played a gentle game of cricket, and the afternoon drifted away. The evening drew slowly in and brought a light breeze with it. A couple of the lads disappeared in the four-wheel drive and came back with a pile of wood. An hour later there was a roaring fire. We sat around the fire savouring, remembering, talking and laughing about the day. We'd played, talked, eaten and drunk. Most of all we'd relaxed. The glow of the sun was on our skin and the heat of the fire was in our bones. We drew closer to the fire as the mild breeze freshened, a quietness sinking upon us. We were a group around a fire, individually lost in our own thoughts, wishing for better times. The beach patrol came by and you could see the longing in their eyes too. They waved and wished, sensing our mood. I could feel the tears starting to well up, but pushed them down. I rubbed the icicle in my chest, which seemed to grow larger and burn brighter in a cold sort of way. I realized years later that if I had cried the icicle would have melted. I wondered if I should report sick with it. It didn't seem to affect my physical performance, but it had an odd emotional presence. I broke the spell. Just as the first sob engulfed me.

"Anyone for a sing song?" I shouted.

We started with Music Man. "I can play the pick your nose, pick your nose, pick your nose. I can play the pick your nose, pick pick pick your nose. Oh, pick pick pick pick pick your nose," we all chorused while picking our noses. Chris Rigger jumped up. "I can play the Nicky Lauder, Nicky Lauder, Nicky Lauder. I can play the Nicky Lauder rah rah rah rah rah." We all leapt up, started slapping our heads and joined in the chorus. "Ouch ouch my head's on fire, my head's on fire, my head's on fire, my head's on fire. Ouch oouch my head's on fire rah rah rah rah rah." "White Cliffs of Dover; Pack Up Your Troubles In Your Old Kit Bag. Oh Sir Jasper Do Not Touch Me," where one word of the line is deleted after each chorus.

"Oh Sir Jasper do not touch me!
"Oh Sir Jasper do not touch!!!!!
"Oh Sir Jasper do not!!!!!!!!!!!
"Oh Sir Jasper doooo!!!!!!!!!!!!
"Oooh Sir Jasper!!!!!!!!!!!!!!!!!!!
"Oooh Siiiirrrr!!!!!!!!!!!!!!!!!!!!!!!
"Ooohhhhh!!!!!!!!!!!!!!!!!!!!!!!!!!!"

We finished off the sing song with Old McDonald's Farm. Two of the girls leapt up and did the first verse. They sang, "And on that farm he had some cows eh ya eh ya ho." When the chorus came they put one of their hands behind their head and the other hand on their hip. The girls then wiggled their hips from left to right and went into the chorus. We all leapt up and joined them and sang. And the cows were cowing it here, and the cows were cowing it there, cowing it here, cowing it there, cowing it everywhere, while knocking our hips together with the person next to us and holding a hand on our hip and one behind our head. The next verse was the rams ramming it here and ramming it there and ramming it everywhere. We all leapt up again, put our hands on our hips and thrust our hips forwards and backwards. Pullets were pulling it here and pullets were pulling it there, pulling it here, pulling it there, pulling it everywhere. Some of the lads bragged a bit because they mimed pulling their willie with two hands which were wide apart and raising their hands high into the sky. The most outrageous one was next. The turkeys were gobbling it here and the turkeys were gobbling it there. Some people thrust their tongue into the inside of their cheek and pushed it out, while doing the actions!! Everyone put one hundred and ten percent into the sing song and every single person was roaring with laughter. It was belly-aching side-splitting stuff.

We sat down exhausted and edged in closer to the fire as the chill sea breeze curled around our bodies. Externally we wanted to look carefree. Underneath we wept.

One of the lads banked up the fire and flames licked into the air once again. The heat felt luxurious on our exposed sun-tanned skin, but now we had to edge back or fry. Dave Clerk from HQ stood up. He walked back a few paces, then ran at the fire. At the last minute he dived through the flames and did a forward roll on the other side. We yelled and cheered as he stood up, arms outstretched like an Olympic gymnast. Somebody else followed and soon there was a queue. One by one they dived through the flames, finishing off with arms outstretched as we yahoo-ed and yelled. Brad staggered to his feet, and Wendy tried to stop him, but it was no use. He'd got his imaginary green lid on. He stepped, or should I say staggered back from the fire while we hooted and yelled, egging him on. He paused for effect, typical marine, then launched himself forward. The shouting died. Bets were being placed as to whether he would make it or not. It was just before the dive through the flames he tripped. People drew back and scattered as a big whoosh of embers flew into the sky and scattered all around. The lads roared. They were going to leave him there, or were too pissed to care. I dragged him out, laughing at the situation. I parked him next to Wendy and checked him over. His eyebrows, moustache and hair were practically gone. He went quiet and buried his right hand in the cool sand.

"Let me know if you're worried and I'll get him back to the medical centre," I told Wendy.

Paul Bleep from South brought the four-wheel-drive Subaru over and tied a pallet behind it.

"Anybody fancy a ride?" he asked.

Two of the lads jumped onto the pallet, knelt down and gripped the cross sections. We crowded behind and watched.

"Ready?" asked Paul.

"Yeah," they replied.

Two columns of sand spumed into the air as the rear wheels spun. The lads on the pallet got sand-blasted, and their bodies became more rigid as they gripped tighter. The pallet bucked into the air and they were off. They zig-zagged down the beach as first one front corner of the pallet dug into the beach and then the other. They were being jerked left then right and they clung on for dear life. Eventually they were pitched off at about twenty miles an hour. Two by two their bodies were discarded along the beach. Towed and tossed off like jetsam. They returned holding their bruised bodies, all with the same exclamation, "Fucking hell!"

Chris and I jumped on. We glanced at each other and smiled. The Subaru set off and the bastards drove along the edge of the incoming tide. We could hear the whoops and laughter increase from the crowd as two fountains of water rose from the rear wheels. This was really dangerous. If we were bucked off forward, which could happen if both corners of the pallet dug in at the same time, we would smash our skulls on the back of the wagon and then we would be hit by the pallet following us. If they had applied the brakes we would have smashed our skulls on the back of the wagon.

WHO GIVES A FUCK!

LETS FUCKING DO IT!

Chris disappeared first, not because he'd lost his grip, but because the strip of wood he was hanging onto came away. He seemed to be sucked upwards and backwards. Disappearing over my right still holding the plank. The end of the plank just missed my face and I can still picture the two protruding nails. I decided to go one better (as you do, as Chris would have said). I stood up, stretched my arms and surfed. It felt so exhilarating racing along in the moonlight with the wind whistling around my ears and the beer buzzing around my brain. Then the pallet hit a bump and I was flying through the air. The flight seemed to be in slow motion, going on for ever. The world had slowed down to allow me the full enjoyment of flight, I thought.

SPLAT. Back to earth.

I tried to raise myself off the beach with my right hand, but I wasn't allowed. My shoulder was giving me grief and I couldn't work out why, so I looked down. A small hillock had suddenly appeared between my neck and my shoulder. I leaned to my left and moved my arm. The hillock between my neck and arm socket moved and it hurt. I sobered instantly and put my injured arm across my chest, supported it with my other arm and walked back to the fire. Kev Wheels moaned light-heartedly about missing all the fun when I said I needed a lift back to the medical centre. I wasn't alone. Two of the other lads who had been on the pallet came as well. One had a broken finger and the other had broken a big toe. I said goodbye to everybody, told Jean and Jane to stay as long as they liked and went.

The doctor was a typical army doctor, caring, sensitive and sympathetic. He pulled us all into his surgery at the same time and sat there laughing as we told him.

"We were playing volleyball," I explained. "I jumped for a high ball at the same time as Tony. The ball caught the end of his finger and broke it. He knocked me off balance and I fell to the ground. I landed on Keith's big toe and broke it. I bust my shoulder at the same time."

"This is one for the party when I get back," he said sympathetically, showing great concern! He dealt with all of us at the same time and prescribed the same treatment. He gave us identical pills and said,

"Take one of these every four hours and report back on Monday morning. There's nothing I can do now."

The more the alcohol wore off the more it hurt. Every bump in the road caused pain with the bone wobbling freely inside my shoulder. I arrived home and tried to get undressed, but couldn't without sickening pain. I left it. I decided to wait until the bruffin kicked in and Jean came home. She would help.

They came in bubbling and bursting to talk. One would start a sentence and the other would butt in. Then the sentence would be hijacked back as they rushed on excitedly to tell me about it.

"The tide was coming in," said Jean.

"Tony Tech got the Subaru stuck," interjected Jane, and she carried on. "Everybody, including the girls, tried to push the Subaru out but it was stuck."

"Somebody went to get your rigger's van and tied a rope between your van and the Subaru," said Jean, with Jane interrupting. Jean just couldn't compete and sat down, leaving Jane to it.

"Every time the rigger's van tried to go forward it went deeper into the sand and the tide was coming in fast. Somebody came up with the bright idea of bringing two more vehicles over. They were on dry sand to begin with. But the tide came in underneath them and they got stuck." Jane had to rest for a minute; it was all too exciting for her. She couldn't wait, and continued breathlessly. "Four vehicles got stuck at the same time," she paused momentarily. "They were really lucky," she continued. "A patrol came by, and they managed to recover all the vehicles, Dad." She paused again, just for a second. "Except yours. The tide was half way up it when we gave in. So it might not even be there in the morning." Jane sat down, panting and giggling. Jean continued.

"We just stood there watching it disappear. Nobody could do anything," she said, all serious, holding her hand to her mouth at the gravity of the situation. Then she burst out laughing again.

"Somebody said we'll get shit from the rigger for this. Who's going to tell him?' Jane chirped in. Then she collapsed again.

I was only too glad to see the back of that van. The lads had done me a favour. Luckily for the driver it was still there the next day. Spanners managed to recover it and tow it back. Jean suddenly remembered.

"How's your shoulder?" she asked. I couldn't resist it.

"It only hurts when I laugh."

6

CROSSMAGLEN

It had been a painful weekend. I couldn't sleep on my right shoulder, and it would be another ten months before I could spend a whole night lying on it.

I took a sickie Monday morning,

"Report to the gym for physio every Tuesday and Thursday," said the doctor. I was only in his surgery two minutes. At work everybody was talking about the wild BBQ we'd had. People were coming up and trying to pat me on the back to say thanks for such a brilliant do. I would pre-empt them by raising my left hand over my right shoulder and say "Watch my shoulder!" They would look at me wonderingly and then reply, "O yeah, I heard about that," and start laughing.

Paul YoS came into the office to see what the score was.

"No rigging for a while," I told him.

"Is Chris capable of carrying out tasks by himself?" he asked.

"Yes, but he'll need someone to show him around," I emphasized.

Chris came in with the coffee. "How's your shoulder?" he asked.

"It fucking hurts," I told him.

We relived Saturday with Brian hanging on to every word. We went through the whole day, every detail. We prompted each other to tell different parts. It was Brian's kind of party and he was pissed off he'd missed it.

I told Chris what was happening concerning him and asked him to keep me informed so that I could check to see they weren't asking too much of him.

Wheels phoned to say the rigger's van was back in camp. However, it was no use to man nor beast. I asked if they could come up with a fast replacement and left them to it. Wheels phoned back half an hour later to say that they had phoned the detachments and that they had come up with a Hiace van. Would that be OK? It was. The driver who had got the rigger's van stuck was frantically cleaning it up. He was trying to get rid of the seaweed and sand so that it would be judged mechanically beyond repair on inspection. He was hoping the story of the BBQ hadn't filtered through to the inspecting officer. Fat chance.

Tie up the loose ends then go, I told myself. My shoulder began to ache again so I popped another bruffin. Home was so welcoming that night. Bed was all I could think about, but it was too early. I wouldn't sleep. By ten o' clock though I was ready. Jean came up. She helped me undress, then it was into the bathroom to wash my body and wince at my shoulder. Another bruffin followed, then a crawl into bed, hoping that sleep would come quickly.

Physio the next morning and the physiotherapist was just what I expected – a fit physical training instructor and a right bastard. He was giving a young lad a hard time as I walked in. We had a similar injury except he'd acquired his playing rugby. "Good morning," I said.

The physio turned round and smiled at me with that another victim look on his face. "What's your problem then?" he asked. I told him.

He set up an exercise exactly the same as the young lad's. It consisted of a rope threaded through a pulley with a small weight on one end. All I had to do was keep pulling the end of the rope and raising the weight up and down. *This hurt.*

The loose bone in my shoulder moved and rubbed on the inside of my flesh as my arm went up and down. I was told that callouses had to form on the inside of my shoulder, to allow the floating bone movement without causing pain. Movement was very limited to begin with, maybe a foot. But I was determined to get back to one hundred percent, and quickly. I drove myself on until sick with pain, sweat bursting over my forehead, then I packed it in. Not able to take any more, I walked the long way back to my office to get rid of that sickening feeling. There was a slight breeze blowing. It cut through my shirt, entered the loose bone through the end and chilled the inside. It made my body shiver and sickened me even more – a lousy feeling. Back in the office I looked at the mound of paperwork that had accumulated over the past few weeks. I wasn't going to be idle. The next four weeks passed quickly. I eliminated the mound of paperwork while regularly visiting the physio. My arm was becoming more mobile and I was now able to dress myself. My exercises were far beyond the young lad's, and the physio drove him on, reducing him to tears as he compared him to an old man like me. It was for his own good, but I don't suppose he thought that.

I was itching to get out and started going out with Chris as support. You weren't allowed out of camp unless you were one hundred percent fit. I hadn't quite reached that stage yet, but there was no way they were going to stop me.

On one outing I climbed into the car and caught the end of my loose shoulder bone on the roof. It brought tears to my eyes and that sick feeling returned. Chris was talking about not going out as he looked at my ashen face. I said, "No way. I'll have to get used to it." A couple of weeks later it seemed to improve dramatically, so I binned the physio and started climbing.

Two jobs came up, one at Crossmaglen and one at Foxholes. The only way in or out was by air. I wanted cloudy nights at these locations to reduce the odds. I checked the weather forecast and we were in luck. Rain was predicted for the next few days, so I booked the choppers and informed all concerned. Ray Tech was coming along and there was no way I could leave Chris out – he was loving it. I booked the choppers for Tuesday and Thursday. This would give us prep and recovery time.

We set off at two on Tuesday afternoon for the heli-pad at Bessbrook Mill. We'd allowed double the time to get there in case of delays, but the journey was smooth and uneventful. We came over a hill and there stood Bessbrook. It was one of those old stone mills that silently dominate the skyline. It cast a mantle that over-powered the surrounding area. It repelled you and gave off an aura of evilness. Your spirit sagged at the sight of Bessbrook. I pitied the poor souls who had to live in this shithole for six months. We turned off the main road and drove down a small lane leading into the mill. There were three concrete walls at the entrance, two on the left and one between them on the right. The right one jutted out between those on the left to form a chicane. It prevented terrorists driving by and shooting the gate guards. We entered the chicane of walls and had to stop in between them. A chain of spikes lay across the road. A soldier eyeballed us through a slit. Deathly silence reigned. We sat and waited for checks to be carried out. It got to you slightly, especially with that weapon pointing through the slit and a pair of nervous eyes behind it. You felt that if you talked the spell would be broken and the weapon would open up. We said nothing. After what seemed to be an eon a soldier appeared round the end of the concrete wall closest to the mill and asked for IDs.

The chopper pad was on the right of the road going through the mill, with the car park next to it. We parked up and reported in to the naval senior rating in the flight office. We cracked a joke between us about him being a long way from sea, while he took details and ran through flight procedures.

"Be here half an hour before take off with all your kit ready to go," he said.

We had two hours to waste in this god-forsaken place, and there was nothing to do. I can't remember anything good to say about Bessbrook. It was the pits. We meandered through the buildings, passing the time, and stumbled across their accommodation. I use the term accommodation very, very loosely. The room had bare oil-stained floorboards and walls with paint peeling off. The grey furniture, which you wouldn't find dead in a second-hand shop, consisted of steel bed frames. A fat, long, shiny, dark green sleeping bag lay on each bed, giving the room the appearance of a slug in-cubator. A steel locker with a dead suitcase on top stood next to each bed. Against the backdrop of nothingness, the beds looked miniaturized, as though dwarfs slept there.

Everything lay dormant. Not a thing moved in this huge caver-nous room that was once so noisy with weaving and spinning machines. All the windows had been whitened to allow light to filter through, but to prevent terrorists firing in. When Ray spoke his voice had no ring. The words were dull and distant. They seemed to be sucked in, absorbed and devoured by the huge emptiness.

"I'd go mental if I had to spend six months in this place," he said.

The three of us were glad to get out of that inhuman, drab room, and our spirits picked up as we distanced ourselves. How did they live there and remain sane?

Ray and I stood next to the equipment while Chris took the van back. He returned five minutes later and we stood assembled, with kit, waiting. A sergeant standing next to a chopper shouted, "Bring your gear over."

We lugged it and stowed it under his supervision, then went back to our original spot and waited. Power was fed into the chopper motor and the whir grew louder, shriller and more intense. The blades started to rotate slowly to begin with, then picked up speed until they all blurred into one. The pilot looked back through his window and gave the thumbs up to the sergeant.

"Come on," shouted the sergeant, waving his arm.

We boarded and sat facing the door as the sergeant clipped a line hanging from the roof to the harness he was wearing. The engine reached full pitch after he spoke into his microphone and we quickly rose into the air. As soon as we were clear of the buildings the pilot did a sharp right and shot forward catching all three of us unaware. A tickle of fear crept up my arse as I grabbed hold of the seat to prevent myself falling out of the open door. Chris and Ray must have had the same tickle. We looked at each other and mouthed, "Fucking hell."

The sergeant turned around and looked at us, smiling. He didn't say anything. He didn't have to. He could see by the look on our faces that they'd achieved what they'd set out to do – put the shits up us. It was tactical flying all the way since the IRA had downed one of their choppers. It was exhilarating, with no warnings of manoeuvres. The big bird would suddenly rise or drop, or bank right or left to give us sinking and rising feelings in our stomachs. We clung to our seats as the pilot did a tight circle round

Crossmaglen, checking for possible terrorist activity before hovering over the camp. He hovered only momentarily to check his position, worrying about blades and nearby buildings. It made contact with the ground. The pilot adjusted its blade pitch and kept its engine revs high, should a fast ascent be needed. The sergeant's movements now became commands. He jerked his finger at us, then his thumb at the door. We leaped out, scurried backwards and forwards under the prop wash, off-loading the equipment. There was no hesitation. As soon as the last bit of kit was off, the chopper rose sharply, catching Ray in the down-draught. Instead of trying to fight it, he just knelt there and waited. After the noise and excitement of the flight, we were left with the total opposite – no noise, no movement, and not a person in sight.

The sergeant major appeared at the door as we carried the kit across. He'd been pre-warned and knew the unit we were from. He didn't ask any questions, showed no interest. Just led us into a small room where we'd set up,

"If there are any problems give me a shout," were his only words. Then he disappeared.

Everywhere we went soldiers stared at us. Not suprising really as we were in civvies, in Crossmaglen, and had come in on a special flight. They were clueless as to who we were or what we were doing, and could only guess. It was seventeen hundred and we had to sit around until early morning when we felt the time would be right to climb. We were hungry. So, leaving the equipment (it just looked like grey boxes), but taking the holdall with the support weapons in, we made our way to the cookhouse. Most cookhouses are warm and clammy. This one was no different. The room silenced as we took our jackets off and sat down. Whispers sprang up all around. Squaddies pointed at us in our civvies and long hair and shoulder-holstered pistols. Ray, Chris and I looked at each other, and smiled.

"We'll keep them guessing aye," said Ray.

An officer came over after we'd eaten and asked, "How was the food?"

"The peas were hard," I said.

"Tell the chef then," he said.

93

The chef was stood behind the hot plate so I shouted over, "Hey chef?" He looked up. "The peas were hard," I told him.

"I know," he replied. How do you get out of that?!

The holdall seemed to draw the most attention as we left. It was zipped tight and straining on its handles. The diner's eyes followed it. We gave Ray a lift to install his equipment, then dozed or read books and let time drift by, as only a squaddie knows how.

Chris's musical watch alarm woke us at two.

"Stay where you are," he said. "I'll get a brew on."

Outside it was patchy cloud, with the moon peeping through now and again, highlighting everything. We sipped coffee and smoked while I outlined what I thought was the best way to climb. I asked Chris if it sounded okay and if he could improve on it. He agreed that he would run up and clamp the antenna on, while I did the zipping. We ran the feeder out in a straight line, making sure it wouldn't snag on anything during the climb. Ray would be on the ground anyway. He could sort any problems. But we didn't want any. We stood waiting for a large cloud to cover the moon with our belts on, right tools and equipment attached. A soldier walked by and said, "You're not going up there, are you?" We nodded. He said the usual.

It went dark as a small cloud drifted over the moon. Chris looked at me. I shook my head. We'd be caught with our pants down if we'd gone then.

"That's the one," I said, pointing toward a larger cloud coming along. We would still have to shift, especially with the stiff breeze scudding the clouds along at a fast pace. But this was a good opportunity. That unreal feeling came over me as I looked up. The tower was moving, not the clouds. A hint of dizziness passed through me. It was still dark and the moon hidden, but getting lighter as the first cloud passed. The edges of the cloud became silver-tipped as the moon shone through. Eventually it revealed itself and blinded us with its brilliance. I looked away to shield my eyes and to recover from the dizziness. Ray and Chris did too. I looked up again as the moon began to hit the strands of loose cloud around the main body of the larger one.

"Ready?" I asked. Chris nodded. "Let's go!"

We set off up the mast in what appeared to be daylight and got to just below wall height.

"Wait, Chris," I said. The moon began to disappear for the second time. It darkened. "Go," I said.

We were off, speeding up the mast, Chris one side and me on the other. No matter who you were climbing with, it was always a race, and I'd never lost. One person had drawn with me, John Tech. He was probably faster since he'd had his hair parted. I stood at the top, one leg hooked over a rung, waiting for Chris to climb the two rungs he was behind. I didn't move until he'd belted off.

CLICK. I was off down the mast. I zipped the feeder cable to a leg, leaving enough slack to allow Chris to clamp the antenna to the mast. The sequence was this. Hook one leg over a rung and tuck your toe under the opposite rung. Zip three times. Down six rungs. Hook one leg over a rung and tuck a toe under the opposite rung. Zip three times. I was flying down, zooming. I reached the twenty-foot level before Chris joined me. We jumped off. I released the suppressed fear by laughing and Ray joined in. The squaddie who had passed by earlier must have been standing in the shadows, watching. He walked by,

"Mad bastards!" he said.

We ran the feeder into the equipment room, soldered on a connector and left Ray to test. It was all over, done with, out of the way, except for the three-hour wait for the chopper. Not wanting to be late we stagged on (Time spent on guard duty watch). We rotated with forty-five minutes on stag and one and a half hours off. This allowed time for breakfast.

We stood at the side of the square with our kit, waiting for the chopper. We weren't alone. Six soldiers were with us. They were vibrant, bubbly, and chatted excitedly. Glad to get out of this hole. We heard it approaching and looked up, but couldn't see anything. It was coming in low and from a different direction to the one we'd arrived – an irregular pattern. It surprised us by creeping in just over the security wall. One second an open peaceful sky, the next a sky full of roaring helicopter. We waited for the sergeant to signal. Then we rushed forward, putting our kit on board. We had that much kit it took two dashes. We leapt on board just as the chopper rose and sat down. Well, we didn't sit down. We had no choice really. We were thrown down onto the bench seats as the chopper catapulted into the air and banked left. The six squaddies were in an A1 mood at getting out of that place. They were laughing, joking and talking about the good times that lay ahead. Not for long though. They sensed the hostility emanating from the back. He sat there, head bowed, avoiding eye contact and conversation, a wreck of a man, drained and dirty, tense and still, but still with adrenalin pumping. He wanted to get rid of the aggression inside him. But this was the wrong place. He'd been out in the field who knows for how long. He'd been picked up on the way over. I didn't recognize him. I thought about making conversation, but changed my mind.

Back at Bessbrook it was straight into the van and head for home.

"What about meeting at ten on Thursday morning?" I asked Ray. "It'll give us plenty of time to get everything ready." He agreed.

Jean was in the kitchen making breakfast when I got home.

"Fancy something to eat?" she asked.

"No thanks, but a cup of tea would go down well," I said. I needed a shower and headed for the bathroom. Jane was in there.

"Hi Dad. I'll be out in five minutes," she called as I tried the door.

I knew how long a woman's five minutes was, so I decided to go down for that cuppa. Fifteen minutes later, "The bathroom's free Dad."

I gave Jean a hug and asked her to wake me at four. I passed Jane on the stairs and gave her a kiss and said, "Have a good day." I showered, scrubbed my teeth and jumped into bed.

Jean shook me gently at four. "Dinner's ready," she whispered.

I washed, dressed and went down. Jane was beaming. She couldn't wait to tell me about the .22 shooting she'd done that afternoon.

"We had a competition this afternoon and guess who won?" she said, pointing proudly to a statuette on top of the fireplace.

"Great. What are you doing tomorrow?" I asked.

"Archery," she replied. I hummed the theme tune to the Robin

Hood series while pretending to draw an arrow from a quiver on my back, stringing it onto a bow and then firing it.

"Come and get it," shouted Jean.

I was famished and tore into it. In between mouthfuls I asked Jane if it was this Saturday that she was going to the adventure training camp.

"Yeah, and I'm really looking forward to it," she said.

"What activities have you got your name down for?" I asked.

"All of them," she replied.

Jean was due a breast cancer check. She wasn't having any problems, but her mum had had it so she was screened on a regular basis. Her appointment had come through for a date in three weeks time at the Royal Victoria Hospital on the Falls Road. She asked if I would take her.

"Remind me on Monday and I'll check out the procedure," I said. "I've too much on this week."

Thursday morning we met at the tech workshops at ten and discussed the job for tonight. Chris was talking as though he was coming with us.

"Hang on Chris. There's only Ray and I going on this job. You're on leave tomorrow and your flight's at one."

"I'll still have time to make it," he said. I put my foot down.

"If the weather comes in, you could be stuck there for days," I told him.

He gave us a lift with the loading while humming and ahh'ing. He said nothing. This time we loaded the stores into a Cavalier, worked out a different route as far as we could, then agreed to meet at two.

"Have a good leave Chris," I said before we left. He walked away with a sad on, hands in pockets and shoulders bowed.

We met at two, drew the weapons and went through the booking-out procedures. We checked the radio and were off, heading down the M1 to Portadown.

"The same car's been behind us since we joined the M1, and it's made no attempt to pass," I told Ray. We were travelling at just below seventy miles an hour. It wasn't unusual to have a car behind you at this speed, but that odd feeling that something doesn't feel right had crept into me. We continued and left the M1 at junction eleven and drove along the short M12 to Portadown. The car was still behind us, but two vehicles away now. Coming up to a large roundabout, I waited for an opening in the traffic, then pulled out. I drove past the road we wanted, did a complete circle of the roundabout and then took the road we should have taken on the first attempt. The car that had been tailing us was now three cars in front, it's occupants relaxed. The cars between us peeled off, leaving the two of us on the road to Newry. We sat back feeling we had the upper hand if there was a contact. Whoever they were, they were going the same way. Someone was transmitting to control and we heard the description of our car and registration being broadcast. I was puzzled. Ray clicked on straightaway and started to laugh. He said the car in front contained two operators and was part of The Unit. I pressed the transmit button and started to give the registration number and description of the car in front, ending the message with "If the passenger would like to turn round and give us a smile, we'll give him a wave." There was no outward response. We didn't expect one. The car sped up and disappeared. We joked about the possibility of a contact situation and an own goal. If there had been a delay or mistake in feeding the cars' descriptions into the central computer, who knows what might have happened.

Bessbrook came into view and once again this ugly monstrosity repelled me. Back through the chicane, park up in the same car park and book in. The sailor gave the same instruction as last time, "Be here half an hour before your flight time," he said.

We must have been getting used to the tactical flying. It wasn't half as exhilarating as the first time. After twenty minutes in the air, the loadmaster closed the door through which we'd climbed aboard and opened the one on the other side. We couldn't see what was going on or where we were. So sat tight waiting for instructions. The chopper stopped descending and began manoeuvering sideways. It didn't settle. It just hovered as the loadie (load-master) waved us out. We had to jump six feet to the ground. Once outside, we understood why. To give some protection the pilot had partially hidden the chopper beside a small hillock. The blades were very close to the upper ground. Had we exited from the other door, we would have been lobotomized.

The soldier receiving us stood very close. Too close, and I began to wonder about his sexual leanings. We were totally aware of his presence. He didn't speak. Wouldn't have heard him anyway. He just stood there. Very close. Waiting. There were no niceties. As soon as the last piece of kit was handed over, the soldier grabbed our sleeves, dragged us down into the kneeling position. He kept a firm grip on our sleeves and waited until the chopper had climbed far enough for him to be heard.

"DO NOT GO IN," he emphasized. "CARRY YOUR KIT OVER TO THE GATE AND WAIT."

I looked at the location for the first time as we humped the kit over. It was in the middle of nowhere and surrounded by a high wire-mesh fence. The fence housed a concrete bunker and an eighty-foot mast. That was it. The last piece of kit arrived at the gate and he grabbed our sleeves again. Serious thoughts this time. What did they do to occupy themselves out here! He tugged our sleeves. We followed into the compound.

"Do not go near those trip wires. They're attached to clay-mores," he said, pointing, then released us. I was more worried about him than the claymores. We went back to the gate, picked up our kit and carried it into the bunker. There were two rooms in the bunker, an observation room and a kitchen. The name kitchen was very loosely attached. Water came from a container, gas from a bottle and food from a tin. The observation room had concrete walls with slits in it, an earth floor, and that was it. To retain your night vision a dim light burned overhead. I never did find the toilet. The soldiers only left the safety of the bunker when they had to. It stank of sweaty bodies, stale cooking smells, shit and urine. It was certainly something you wouldn't find in any Northern Ireland tourist brochure. It had just the basic needs to live. Bessbrook seemed palatial by comparison. The three other soldiers stared as we entered, backed off slightly and gave us space. Rarely did they get visitors, especially in civvies. They would've been told we were arriving, and departing. Nothing else.

"Is there any chance of a brew?" I asked trying to break the ice.

"Sure," said one of the soldiers, suddenly realizing we were from the same planet.

"This is better than the Hilton," I remarked.

"Wait till you see the other guests. They've got four legs," said one of the others.

"I've got to climb the mast in the early hours and fix an antenna," I told them. "And Ray," I said pointing to him, "has to install a piece of equipment in the bunker." I think install is probably the wrong word. There was no power to drill the wall. The equipment would just sit on the floor. "Can you provide cover while I climb?" I asked the corporal. There wasn't a problem.

We dug out our books, read, dozed, ate and drank the time away. There was no wandering about outside. The six of us were cooped up in ten cubic feet. The odd rat popped in to see us. It would stare at us, then scamper off at the first sign of movement.

The corporal shook us at zero two thirty, but we weren't really asleep. We were dozing in that half-sleep half-awake state. I asked him what the situation was like outside.

"There's been no sign of movement, but that doesn't mean anything," he said. "Right, let's get the job out of the way. Can you position your men?"

His lads were already awake, but you were hard pushed to tell. They responded like robots with half-burnt-out circuitry. They'd received their command to stand to. They seemed to know what to do but not how to do it. They'd become zombified by their entombment in this concrete sarcophagus and their brains had dulled. I visualized little sparks in their heads as the command was rejected, passed onto the next cell, rejected. The command finally made contact with the right cell in one of them. He stirred. It drew the attention of the others, whose brains still hadn't worked out what was required from the command to stand to. They gazed as he rose, brains finally engaging. Movement could be detected in their bodies. It seemed to take superhuman effort for them to rise and move to their positions. They stood by their slits, switched on their night scopes, scanned and adjusted. I waited until they came fully alive, fastened on my belt, put the tools, spare nuts and clamp in my pockets, then hung the pouch of zips around my neck. I picked up the coil of cable, looked at Ray and nodded towards the exit. I headed in a straight line to the base of the mast, uncoiling the cable as I went. I double-checked the tools, zipped the antenna to my belt and was ready. It had turned into a clear night. Might as well have been daytime it was so light. The moon was like a giant searchlight beaming down. It revealed every detail in perfect clarity. Trees loomed on the surrounding hills beyond the fence. Bramble bushes could be seen distinctly at two hundred metres. The parts of the concrete bunker not covered by earth seemed to act like giant mirrors and reflected the moon's rays everywhere. There was no hiding and no turning back. The area was alive with animals scurrying and rustling in the undergrowth, calling to each other. If it's going to happen, it's going to happen. I'd often thought about taking a weapon up with me. I'd been through this many times, each time realizing that the only thing I'd want to do if shot at would be to run down. I wouldn't be able to see where the shot came from and the weapon would get in the way on my rush down. I binned the idea, again.

There were two antennae on the mast. No problem finding a position for my antenna and the climb would be easy. Gone were the days of jangling spanners and antennae banging on the mast. My rigging techniques were honed and perfected. No more shaking hands. No more trembling knees. No more breathlessness. Every move and ounce of energy spent were deliberate and directed.

The wildlife sensed the tension in me, went quiet, waited. It took two silent minutes to climb and attach my belt. I removed the antenna, held it in position for clamping, put the nuts on, finger tightened, locked them off with a spanner. Everything was done first time. Just once. No repeats.

I never thought about the possibility of being shot any more. I had reduced the odds as far as I could. There was nothing else I could do to make it safer. If I was shot, I was shot.

There was no contact and no hiccups. The job just flowed. I walked the straightest line possible back to the bunker, aware of the trip wires. Ray poked the cable through a hole in the bunker wall where other cables entered. Then went inside to pull in the slack. I stayed outside to make sure it didn't snag.

A muffled shriek followed by, "Bastard!" came from Ray.

I wasn't going to ask what had happened while I stood out here. He could explain later. But it started me laughing.

"Is that it?" asked the corporal as I entered. I nodded. He stood his men down. Ray appeared from the kitchen, eyes sparkling in the dim light. Something had put the shits up him.

"What was the yell?" I asked.

"I was searching for the cable," he said, moving his hand around to emphasize the action. "You know how dark it is in there. Well there was a rat sat in the corner. But I couldn't see the dam thing." He paused and relived the moment, shuddered slightly. "I must have frightened it, and it ran off brushing itself against my hand." He shuddered again, wiped his hand on his jacket, trying to wipe the feeling away.

We sat on the floor. It was the only place where we could sit. We leaned against the wall. It was the only place where we could lean. The wall sucked out the warmth from our bodies and drove in the cold. It was a restless night. Every half-hour we would wake up, move a numb shoulder around, swop shoulders and doze off again. We all did it.

Ray and I stared into space with blank eyes and blank minds as dawn broke, in serious danger of joining the undead. We could hear the water boiling. It registered in the back of our brains, but the front part ignored it. We sat dormant, staring, spaced out. The smell of tea brewing wafted in. I gulped and my brain became alert once more. I could taste it going down my throat. When it arrived, I hugged the cup with both hands, drew the heat into my body. It tasted and felt like the elixir of life. I took small sips. I tried to make it last for ever. I savoured every millilitre. My thoughts drifted to the bed I would soon be climbing into. It caused my shoulders to move backwards and forwards, one at a time. An involuntary "Umm" came from my lips as I imagined snuggling down under the quilt after a night in this shit hole – sheer luxury.

We could hear the chopper approaching. There was activity. Everybody manned their posts to give covering fire should it be needed. We had to be in a position for loading as the chopper landed. This was to minimize its vulnerability on the ground. The corporal's requests became urgent.

"Come on," he said, grabbing a piece of our kit and heading for the exit. I gulped the last bit of my tea and felt a warm glow as the tea made its way down into my stomach. Then I followed.

The chopper varied its approach and changed its landing at will. The three of us stood at the gate, waiting to see where it would land. It came down on the other side. Grunting and running, we heaved our kit round, threw it on board and followed.

The contents of my stomach lurched to my throat as the chopper shot into the air. It was as though it had been fired from a huge cannon. It drove my legs upward and into my hips. I watched through the open door, watched a small speck. The corporal. He ran round the bunker urgently, in fear of his life. He had come to life for ten minutes. Now he was entering the trolls' cave, to be turned into stone once again.

The only thing you want to do when you return to base is go to bed. *But,* you have to book in and unload the weapons. You have to empty the magazines and the car. *Then* you can go home. Even *then* it hasn't finished. You need a shower. You need to scrub your teeth, and you need a drink. *Then* you can climb into that bed that you've spent the whole night thinking about. The tasks seemed to go on for ever, popping up as you go along, trying to prevent you from going to that bed.

"Can you phone Paul YoS? Let him know how the job went?" said Tony Bleep as I unloaded the magazines.

"*No, I fucking can't,*" was my first thought.

You know it has to be done, so you do it. Trying to sound cheerful isn't easy, especially when the person at the other end leans out of his warm bed to answer the phone, but you deal with it. You go home and want a shower. Jane's in the bathroom and I have to wait ten minutes. It seems like an hour. The world is against you.

All I want to do is go to fuckin' bed!! But you have to wait. Plod on. Jane comes out. I go in. I undress, wash, and the feeling is heaven as a thick layer of dirty skin seems to be peeled off my body, leaving me all rosy, pink and tingling. I can now wander into the bedroom. To that warm, soft, woman–perfume–scented bed that my wife has just climbed out. It had seemed a thousand miles away, but now it's there. Finally you crash out, leaving the world to carry on without you.

7

COALISLAND

I checked out the procedure for Jean's visit to Victoria Hospital on the Falls Road and it turned out I had two options. I could go in uniform with an armed guard and travel in a military vehicle or I could wear civvies and take another soldier with me in civvies, drop Jean off for her appointment, then come back and pick her up. I got the map out, checked the route then phoned Ray.

"Ray, are you busy?"

"No. Is there a problem?"

"Not really. Jean's got an appointment at Victoria Hospital soon. I just wanted to check out the route. Do you fancy a ride?"

"Sure. What time are you planning on leaving?"

"Ten minutes. OK?"

"That's fine. Come and pick me up."

The journey ended in a cul-de-sac that led to the hospital. At the end of the cul-de-sac was a large square car park that squatted in front of the hospital. A road ran round the car park, which passed in front of the entrance. I studied the surroundings and felt at ease.

I outlined the options to Jean over lunch and asked her what she thought.

"What do you think?" she asked.

"I think it would be better to blend in. The only time anyone would know you weren't Irish is when you spoke. The only time you have to speak is when you report to reception. Take a book with you and keep your nose in it. People will ignore you."

"What should I do if I'm concerned?"

"Get in touch with the staff. When you've had your appointment give me a ring and I'll pick you up. Make sure there's nobody within hearing distance when you call. If you feel compromised in any way tell me you will meet me inside the hospital entrance. I'll come in, walk past you and check things out, but don't let on. If I don't like the situation I'll walk out and get in touch with control. If you feel everything is OK, tell me you'll meet me on the corner of the car park. Which one do you feel most comfortable with?"

"I think it would be better if you dropped me off and picked me up."

I logged Jeans visit with the relevant departments, then popped into Paul YoS' and Jim FoS' office.

"Got a good speech lined up for your farewell?" I asked Jim.

I got his usual grunt. Paul was writing, head bowed with his lip in the usual half-smirk position, "What a cheerful bunch these are," I thought.

"I'm going to take the afternoon off," I said to no one in particular. "The trees at the bottom of the garden are blocking the light and need pruning. I'll be at home all afternoon if anybody needs me."

They both looked up with a 'you never asked me' look on their face, but said nothing. All they did was sit in their office on their fat arses and work a normal day. There was no way I was going to *ask* for time off with all the hours I was putting in. I walked out and left them sulking.

I was up a tree in the garden, merrily cutting away and relaxing when I heard a voice.

"I've been trying to contact you on your bleeper all afternoon. Aren't you wearing it?" I turned and there was Jim FoS.

"Is there a problem?" I asked.

"I wanted to ask you some questions about that last job you went on."

"Fire away," I said, and carried on pruning.

The questions he asked were so trivial they could have waited until next year. It was obvious he was trying to show who's boss. He got right up my fucking nose.

"Fancy sharing your farewell with Jim FoS?" I said to Roy the next day.

"He's never bought anybody a drink since he arrived," Roy told me. "I'll bet you he doesn't get his hand down," he said.

I told Roy what had happened the previous afternoon with Jim.

"That man," he said, shaking his head in disbelief. "He's always going on at everybody about their bleeper. He went to a meeting in London last year and guess what?" I hunched my shoulders. "He forgot his bleeper. Why doesn't he take a day off?" Roy gave me an idea!

I went to my office and started searching, found what I wanted, then typed Jim FoS's name on an envelope and put it inside. On the paper it said:

WHEN THE LORD MADE MAN, ALL THE PARTS OF THE BODY ARGUED OVER WHO WOULD BE BOSS.

THE BRAIN EXPLAINED THAT SINCE HE CONTROLLED ALL THE PARTS OF THE BODY HE SHOULD BE BOSS.

THE LEGS ARGUED THAT SINCE THEY TOOK THE MAN WHEREVER HE WANTED TO GO THEY SHOULD BE BOSS.

THE EYES SAID THAT WITHOUT THEM MAN WOULD BE HELPLESS SO THEY WANTED TO BE BOSS.

THEN THE ASSHOLE APPLIED FOR THE JOB.

THE OTHER PARTS OF THE BODY LAUGHED SO HARD THAT THE ASSHOLE BECAME MAD AND CLOSED UP.

AFTER A FEW DAYS THE BRAIN WENT FOGGY, THE LEGS GOT WOBBLY, THE STOMACH GOT ILL, THE EYES GOT CROSSED AND UNABLE TO SEE.

THEY ALL CONCEDED AND MADE THE ASSHOLE BOSS.

THIS PROVES THAT YOU DON'T HAVE TO BE A BRAIN TO BE A BOSS . . .

JUST AN ASSHOLE.

Jim never mentioned the note to anybody, but I knew he'd received it. I could see it in his eyes every time he looked at me. That 'I know it was you' look was there. I met Jim in Germany a year later and he gave me that same look, but I didn't let on. Well Jim, if you read my book, you'll know now!

Nobody could see me when I walked into tech workshops in the afternoon, but I was greeted by, "Jack."

I stopped and looked round, caught unaware. Then I remembered the camera.

"Yes Ray," I said, walking into the main workshop.

"Did you hear about Tony Bleep?" he asked.

"No."

"He was on orders for getting the Transit stuck on the beach."

"What happened?"

"He was fined two hundred pounds."

"I thought he'd cleaned it up and was hoping to get away with it?"

"He didn't clean it well enough. The inspecting officer found a lump of seaweed in the engine compartment."

Brad and Frank came over. Glad of a break and a chance to talk to someone from outside the technical workshop.

"I had to jump-start the car this morning. Probably have to buy a new battery," Brad complained.

'When I' is a familiar start to a sentence for a squaddie. The Falkland Islanders nicknamed us 'When eyes'.

"When I," began Frank, "was in Germany we used to jump-start vehicles with one lead," he said, smiling, all knowledgeable.

A thinking frown appeared on Brad's forehead as he tried to work it out. Brad was a very thorough-minded technical person and liked to prove things.

"No," he said. "You will need two jump leads. One from positive to positive and one from negative to negative, or the circuit will be incomplete. No, I don't believe that," said Brad, returning the knowledgeable smile and walking off to his office.

Radio wagons are packed with equipment and use high voltage, and it was not uncommon for the whole vehicle to become live. To overcome this problem a spike would be driven into the ground and a wire attached from the vehicle to the spike. Even then you took further precautions by leaping on or off the vehicle so as not to act as an earth.

"You are talking about jump-starting two radio vehicles, Frank. They would both have had earth spikes in the ground. The two earth spikes would have completed the circuit," I told him. "Why don't you get one up on Brad?"

"Go on," he said, all interested. "I'm listening."

"Park two cars close together. Attach a wire to the earth terminal of one starter motor so he can't see it. Run the wire under the car and out of the back. Then run it under the other car and attach it to its starter motor. Make sure it's black so it will blend in with the car park, and drop some white chippings over it. Then you can just attach the one wire to the battery and it'll start."

Frank pondered, rubbed his chin and walked away.

The bar was packed on Friday.

"I didn't know you were so popular," I said to Roy.

"It's not me. Everybody wants to make sure he goes," he said, jerking his thumb in Jim's direction, "and hopefully get a beer out of him."

Fat chance.

Jim opened his speech with, "I'm going to Germany," and there was an almighty cheer.

"I'm going to apply for UK then," shouted somebody. Another cheer.

"Don't forget your bleeper." Another cheer.

That's all he said. Four words. He couldn't take it and moved to the corner of the bar. He stayed for Roy's speech, and left when he heard Roy say, "The drinks are on me."

Roy brought his replacement over and introduced me.

"Jack, this is Trevor, my replacement."

Trevor was tall, slim and cheerful. We shook hands and were instant friends. Trevor would be dead in three months' time.

"If you ever get fed up of being stuck inside we're always short of riggers," I told him.

"I'll take you up on that," he said. "I get hacked off with being inside all the time."

The drinks flowed, the conversation got louder and the evening started to buzz.

"Hey Rigger," shouted Rob Seven. "Come over here and listen to this." I walked over to his group and waited.

"Go on. Tell him about last night," said Rob.

"Me and Steve went to install some surveillance equipment on the roof of a block of flats in Belfast," said Ron Seven.

Steve and Ron had that wild-eyed look about them, and hadn't wound down yet. The odd drop of spittle escaped Ron's lips as he spoke.

"We parked at the flats and humped the kit up onto the roof."

"That's a bit dodgey, just the two of you on the roof isn't it?" I asked.

"It's not that bad. We can lock the roof door behind us," said Steve, taking up the story. "We'd been at it for about half an hour when I realized I'd left my test meter in the car."

"So I said I'd go and get it," said Ron, and continued. "I locked the roof door behind me. Went down in the lift and was stood looking in the boot when this bloke walks up. 'Are you the squaddie from Lisburn?' he says. 'No, I work for BT,' I told him. 'So do I. What department are you with?' I was fucked. My arse started twitching and I looked around." He and Steve were drawn back to the situation. Their bodies were becoming tense and they moved in unison. They hunched their shoulders at the same time, drank their drinks at the same time and shifted their weight from one foot to the other at the same time. Their eyes sparkled and their minds kept drifting.

"I locked the boot, had another look round and headed back. The guy disappeared around the side of the flats. I was hoping he didn't have any mates round there." He paused again, then continued. "I had to wait for the lift, and it seemed to take hours. I kept looking around, checking all the time, and kept my hand inside my jacket on the pistol grip." He put his hand inside his jacket and kept it there for a few seconds, then withdrew it. "I could hear the creaks and groans of the lift as it came down. I was urging it on, saying fucking hurry up out loud." He paused, lowered his head and chuckled. Then he shook his head, looked

110

up and continued. "The door opened and there was nobody in there. What a relief that was. I had a quick look round before I entered the lift," he said, looking left and right. Steve looked from left to right with him. "I jumped in and I thought the door had jammed it was taking so long to shut. I kept jabbing my finger on the fourteenth button," he said, jabbing his finger. Steve jabbed his finger too.

We'd all been watching Steve mimic Ron and said nothing. I couldn't help it this time and started to laugh; the others joined in.

"What are you laughing at?" asked Ron.

"It's Steve," I said. "Everything you do he does. He's like your doppelganger." Silence.

"What's that?" asked Ron, looking confused.

"It doesn't matter. Get on with the story," I urged.

"Where was I?" he asked, scratching his head.

"In the lift," someone prompted.

"Yeah," he said, throwing himself back into it. "I was really relieved when the door shut. The sweat was pouring out of me, and I had to lean against the wall," he said, wiping his brow. The story was exhausting and exciting him at the same time and he paused for a few seconds. We waited.

"The lift started to slow down at the eighth floor, and my heart jumped into my mouth. Literally," he said leaning forward to emphasize the point. "The door opened and I practically shit myself. There were four youths stood there." He had to pause again. "Thinking back," he continued, "I don't know who was more shocked, them or me. Because I drew my pistol," he said, putting his hand inside his jacket. He then withdrew his hand and pointed his finger at us as though it was the barrel of his Browning. "I pointed it towards them. Cocked it." He ran through the motions of cocking the weapon. "And shouted, 'FUCK OFF'." He rigidly held the pose and sank into a trance. Silence fell about him. He suddenly became all tired. Lowered his arm, and slouched.

"What happened then?" I asked. He was spent, but continued.

"The door shut on it's own and I went up to the fourteenth floor." You could see more tension leave him as he said the sentence.

111

"How'd you get out?" I asked.

"There was no way we were leaving that roof without an escort," said Steve. "I radioed control. Told them what the situation was, and they sent two pigs in. We didn't move until they tapped on the door. There was no way we were leaving that roof without them. The car's still there. It will have to be checked out before it's moved." They were definitely going to make a night of it. I was up early tomorrow, so left them to it.

I dropped Jean and Jane at the airport. I wouldn't see Jane until the next half term so gave her a big hug.

"Got Ralph?" I asked her.

"I never go anywhere without him Dad."

Jean was going to stay with Belinda, our other daughter, for a while.

"Give me a ring when you've booked your return flight," I told her. "And I'll pick you up." Then I headed back to work.

There was a knock on my office door.

"Who's there?" I asked.

"Ray and Jim YoS," said Ray.

"In that case I'm in," I said, standing up to let them in. They came in smiling and sat down.

"What have you got on next Wednesday?" asked Ray.

"What's the job?" I asked.

"We've got to stick a camera on the mast at Coal Island police station and we will probably need some help."

"Coal Island. Dodgy place. We will be entering hillbilly country. You're guaranteed to get shot there. It'll cost you," I said, smiling. "What arrangements have you made?"

"We're going to book three green teams to patrol the ground while we're up. We should be OK," said Ray.

"Fine. I'll be there," I told them.

We passed the green teams as we neared the police station. They'd been dropped off up the road and made their way in on foot. We halted at the gates and waited. Two cars full of men in civvies rattled the patrol commander and as he approached he gave a hand signal. They all knelt down and started to scan. I thought I'd let him know we were on the same side. Make him relax a little, so I opened the window and said, "You're in for a long night tonight." It had the reverse effect. He stiffened, became more vigilant. They followed us in, picked a corner of the yard and parked themselves. We parked under the mast and began to unload.

"Can you unload the kit, lads, while I have a word with the foot patrols?" I said to no one in particular and left them to it. A corporal stepped forward as I neared them.

"Are you in charge?" he asked me.

"Yes."

"What's happening?"

"We have to rig a camera at the top of the tower. It'll take between three and four hours and we'll need ground cover all the time. Would it be possible to have one of your lads on that roof there?" I said, pointing. "So he can scan the rooftops and windows."

"Will you be taking a break or will you be up all the time?"

"We'll be up all the time. Will that be a problem?"

"No."

"It'll take about thirty minutes to set up. There's nothing you can do till then. I'll give you a shout when we're ready."

We'd decided to use the abseil ropes on this one. John tech was laying them out. I gave him a lift and left Ray and Frank to sort out the technical side.

"Ropes out. Equipment ready," I said to John, Frank and Ray who were stood close by. "Got your tools John?"

"Yeah," he said, patting his pockets.

"Anything we might have missed?" I said, doing a final scan. There was no answer. I walked over to the foot patrols.

"We're ready. Can you deploy your men?" They lined up in three single files and waited for the gates to open. Then left at two-minute intervals.

"We'll give them five minutes to fan out, then we're on," I said.

John and I stood at the bottom of the mast, both equally loaded. John had the hauling rope attached to his belt and I an abseil rope. No matter whom you climbed with, it was always a race.

"Ready?" John nodded. We stepped forward, put one foot on the first rung and waited.

"Go," I whispered loudly.

We scooted up the mast, hand over hand, foot over foot, none of us gaining an advantage. The higher we climbed the more rope we hauled and the harder it became. My muscles were letting me know I was pushing it, but I carried on. John must have been going through the same. Our heads rose above the top of the mast at the same time and we looked at each other, smiled, climbed another couple of rungs and belted off. Vapour rose from our over-heated bodies and joined the hot breath being expelled from our lungs. It formed a cloud around us, the only one that night.

"What do you reckon John?"

"Dead heat, you old bastard," he said shaking his head and laughing from the exhilaration. I fed the end of my abseil rope down and Ray tied it off. John raised his on the hauling rope and began sorting himself out. I leaned back in my belt, relaxed, looked around and waited for John.

"OK," John said to me. The radio hung around my neck and nestled inside my jacket. I pulled it out and said, "OK Ray."

The whole of Coal Island probably knew that we were there, but why advertise by shouting? Ray heaved and the first heavy mounting bracket started to rise. Had we let it rise vertically, it would have clanged against every rung. We didn't want to damage the equipment or the mast, or make any noise. So we attached another rope to the bracket. Frank was about thirty feet from the mast, holding the second rope and letting it slip gently through his fingers. He kept just enough tension on it to keep the bracket away from the mast. Too much tension and he would have made hauling difficult.

We watched the bracket slowly rise. It was coming up on John's side and he reached down, grabbed it, eased it away from the mast for the final couple of feet and nodded to me. I pressed the transmit button. "Stop."

Forty minutes later we were ready for the next bit of kit, but it would be ten more minutes before we could haul it. A slight breeze had picked up and the hauling rope and abseil ropes had become entangled. We couldn't see the streets, but we could hear them. There were engines revving, cars accelerating and people shouting. The green teams were having their bottle seriously tested again.

"I'm glad we're up here," I said to John, snuggling down in my jacket and feeling comfortable. Second piece of kit in place and we were at the one and a half-hour point. The breeze had freshened and this time it took fifteen minutes to untangle the ropes. Ray had to assist by climbing half-way up the mast.

"John. We've got three more hauls. If we do this every time we'll add forty-five minutes to the job. And, if we have to abseil down, we'll have to sort the ropes out first. We'll be sitting ducks. What do you reckon?"

"What! Bin the ropes?"

"Yeah. They're useless." A look of concern crossed his face at the thought of losing his fast descent. What fast descent? He saw the reasoning.

"OK. Let's bin 'em."

"Clear the mast. We're dropping the ropes."

We held them at arm's length, down-wind of the mast and let go.

All hell was breaking loose in the streets below. More cars had joined in and the noise level had risen dramatically. I could see the point coming where they would have to withdraw their cover. We worked flat out. We wanted to get out of this place and I'm sure they did too.

We'd been up three and a half hours before the last pieces of kit, the feeder and control cable, started to rise. John zipped them to the mast, then I leaned forward, took my jacket off and put it over our heads. A pinprick of light shone through the taped face of the torch; it was enough. John could have terminated by memory, but we wanted it right first time. No second tries. I held the piece of paper, shone the torch on it and said, "Green on two." Then shone the torch on the termination strip, watched and confirmed, "Blue on five."

You may think this is over the top, but we never had second visits.

"Start testing," I told Ray.

We dropped the hauling rope, recovered the pulley and then made our way down. Testing was always a tense moment, as the cameras didn't travel well. We took precautions now by wrapping them in foam; it seemed to work. If it didn't work we may have had to check the whole system and maybe replace the camera or cable. I would have loved to call in the foot patrols. They were getting a lot of flak out there, but we may have to climb again.

"Yo," yelled Ray as a picture of some house somewhere in Coal Island appeared on the screen.

"I'm going to call the teams in, Ray. Is that OK?"

"Yeah. This is a good picture."

They'd looked reasonably fresh when they'd left the yard. They returned with stress lines etched deep into their faces. They dragged their weary bodies in, made their way to their corner and collapsed. Pulled out their fags and drew deeply.

"We've finished here," said the corporal into the radio.

"We'll be there in fifteen minutes."

"They'll be here in fifteen minutes and it's a ten-minute walk. You've got five minutes," the corporal told them. There were groans, but they were happy groans. Their thoughts would be exactly the same as mine. Show me a bed.

We left a couple of minutes after them and two cars followed us. The one behind was close and had his main beam on; it high-lighted the inside of the car. He probably thought we were civvie contractors and were an easy target. He revved, drove right up our arse, tooted his horn, backed off, then did the same again. I pressed the button and opened my window, waited until he was right up our arse again, then leaned out and pointed the support weapon at him. His car stood on its nose. We drove off laughing.

Home but no bed yet. Ropes entwined round masts, kit being hauled up were in my mind. Headlights were before my eyes. Engines revving, shouting, and radio talk were in my ears. It would be a couple of stiff ones, followed by a couple of stiff ones, before I was ready for bed.

8

BELINDA

I was really enjoying the peace and calm of an empty house. I'd spent Saturday lolling in a deck chair in the garden reading a book. Today, Sunday, was going to be the same. I was mellowing out, laying back, soaking up the UVs with a beer at my side when the phone rang. I felt annoyed and cheated, and wondered whether I should bother answering. A weary sigh escaped as I pushed myself up. I walked in slowly, hoping it would stop before I got there.

"Hello."

"We've got problems Jack," said Jean. "Belinda and Phil have had an almighty bust up. He wouldn't leave our house until I told him to and he said he's coming back for his stuff tomorrow. We've decided it would be better if Belinda came back to live with us in the quarter for a while. Can you come and pick us up?" Phil could be a nasty bastard.

"I'll have to check a few things out. I'll get back to you as soon as possible," I told her.

The covert cars were changed on a regular basis and Wheels were always looking for drivers to take them back. I rang the bell of Robbie Wheels' house and waited. He opened the door and I explained the situation.

"Sierra, Montego or Passat?" he asked.

"Sierra will do fine," I said.

We went down to the office and, while Robbie did the paperwork, I rang Paul YoS.

"Paul, it's Jack."

"Everything OK?"

"Not really. I've got to go back to the mainland to pick up Jean and our daughter. There's a problem with her boyfriend. There's nothing on at the moment. I should be back in three or four days. If anything does crop up, Chris can deal with it. I'll have my pager with me, just in case."

"OK. See you when you get back."

Robbie held out the paperwork and keys.

"Thanks Robbie, I owe you a beer."

"Forget it," he said waving his hand. "Have a good trip."

"I'll be there about two in the morning," I told Jean.

"Oh good. You'll be here when he comes for his stuff."

I stood on the deck and looked up at the silent glittering sky. I felt the gentle roll of the ship and the steady throb of the engines through the rail. The only sound was the lapping of the waves. A feeling of serenity passed through me and I sighed again. I cast my mind back over the last sixteen months. I thought about the experiences I'd gone through and the strain. The latter was starting to show. I wasn't afraid of going into any location; after all, I had visited most. The problem was that even when I wasn't at work I had to remain alert, and it was wearing me down. I felt bone-weary, drained of my zest for life. Even the two weeks' holiday in Lanzarote hadn't done me any good. The only time I'd relaxed was when I was drunk. I looked down. The sea was so inviting. I could just slip over the side into that black moving mass and enter a deep, deep sleep. There'd be no more worries as my body wallowed down there. I'd be pushed by a tide, tugged by a current, and I'd drift around the world. I'd be visiting places I'd never seen before, in total tranquility. The fish would be there, biting off little bits, nibbling, until nothingness.

A cold breeze picked up as we hit the open sea. It wrapped itself around my body and made me shiver. My brain and my body needed resting. The next couple of days could be critical. I sighed, dragged my weary body inside and rested it.

I pulled up outside the house and the lights were on. Jean's face appeared at the kitchen window, then disappeared. She stood at the door, waiting, holding it open for me. I gave her a hug and went in. Belinda was still up.

"Hi Dad. I'm really glad you could make it," she said giving me a hug.

"He's coming back at twelve tomorrow. I mean today, to get his stuff. What shall we do?" I was too tired to think straight and knew it.

"Wake me at nine in the morning. We'll work something out then," I said and headed for bed. I was ZZedding before I hit the pillow. Sleep was instant. '

Half eight and the house was quiet as I trundled downstairs for breakfast. I put the kettle on, made a coffee and sipped it while working out how to deal with the day. I didn't want Phil to enter the house. If violence broke out, and there was a good chance it would, I would be confined and furniture would get damaged. Phil had a small boat on a trailer parked in the driveway. He'd picked it up cheap and was doing it up. Belinda had packed his bags and they stood in the hallway waiting for him. The two thoughts came together.

I could hear my granddaughter Anna-Lisa playing in her bedroom, so I crept up. I slowly opened the door and peered in. A big smile burst across her face and she came towards me with outstretched arms. I turned round and knelt down. She jumped on my back and I carried her down for breakfast. We must have disturbed the rest of the house because ten minutes later Belinda walked into the kitchen, yawning, followed closely by Jean.

"I've put his bags in his boat. There is absolutely no reason why he should enter the house. So no matter what happens, don't let him in," I said, rather too harshly. I softened my voice, "I still have to swop the car, but I won't do that until he's collected his kit. Then we can leave." They were relieved.

The morning drifted and about eleven I looked out of the window. One of the neighbours on the other side of the road was fixing his car. I hadn't seen him for ages so strolled over for a chat. He was lying on the ground with his head under the car and came out when I spoke. We'd been chatting for five minutes when I saw Phil approaching the house. He looked over and I shouted to him,

"Don't go in the house. Your bags are in the boat. You've got twenty-four hours to move the boat. If it's still there after that time, I'll dump it."

I could see his jaw set and his body stiffen. He returned to the end of the drive with his bags, put them down and stood there looking at me. Then he began yelling, "Who the fuck do you think you are? I'm not walking out of here because you say so," and he began walking towards me. He took his jacket off, cast it to the ground, pushed his sleeves up and continued his journey.

"Oh shit," said the neighbour and stepped away.

The kitchen window opened and Jean's head appeared,

"Get in the house now Jack," she shouted. Her voice was shrilled and fear had crept into it. If I backed down now, I would probably have this shithead on my back for the rest of my life. He was taller than me, broader than me and younger than me. I gave him better odds than me in a prolonged brawl. The only way I could win this was to go in first, fast and hard. I was surprised at how calm I was now I'd made my decision. I stood there staring directly into his eyes as he approached, totally silent, totally still, just waiting. My mind was clear and undisturbed as I worked out the best way to drop the bastard. Thinking back, it must have only taken a few seconds for him to cross the road, but I thought about an awful lot. My brain must have been in megadrive, transmitting messages from one section to the other as I thought through the options. I discarded most and settled on one. When he was one step away I would step forward fast, knee him in the balls and poke my fingers into his eyes. I had no remorse about my thoughts. They would happen. Phil was five strides away and my brain began checking my body over. I laughed inwardly as I compared my brain with a computer. My brain was carrying out pre-checks and programming my body. I couldn't believe how natural it felt. I was totally relaxed. My heart was beating at the same rate but harder, and my vision had blurred out everything but *him*. I was even thinking about golf and keeping my eye on the ball. First his nuts then his eyes; he was my total world at this moment. He was three paces away and I still hadn't moved or blinked since he had begun walking towards me. Things were changing slightly. My heart was now beating faster and I could feel adrenalin being forced around my system. I was keyed up with every aspect of my body on full alert. I raised myself onto the balls of my feet. Not that I'd physically thought about it. It just happened. He was now two paces away and he was going down with one more step. Fear appeared in his eyes and he stopped, unsure now of the outcome. He hesitated for a couple of seconds, then began to retreat. He picked up his jacket and made his way back across the road, still carrying on the verbal tirade.

"Don't fucking stare at me like that," he shouted, while pointing at me. "Who the fuck do you think you are?" he continued. He picked his bags up and left. I was elated and realized I'd enjoyed the whole scene. Jean and Belinda were overjoyed. They fussed around and hugged me, made me a coffee and gave me a cigarette. Even Anna-Lisa sensed their mood and joined in by jumping up onto my knee and shouting.

"When can we go?" asked Belinda excitedly.

"I'd prefer to wait until tomorrow. I don't like the idea of him coming back for his boat when the house is empty, and I have to exchange the car," I told her.

"Oh," she said, slightly deflated.

After lunch I went to exchange the car and arrived back five hours later with a Passat. I was still locking the door of the car when they came running out to greet me. They were bouncing and overjoyed and they were all trying to talk at the same time. "He's been to pick up the boat. Can we go now?" they said joyfully.

The last twenty-four hours had been long and hard. I wanted to get some decent sleep, but the look in their eyes!

"OK," I said. "But I need something to eat before we leave."

The further north we drove the worse the weather got. By the time we hit the A75 to Stranraer it was lashing it down. The outside weather enhanced the inside warmth and cosiness of the car. The girls had started off the journey with nonstop chatter, but were now asleep. I cast my mind back over the last twenty-four hours and thought about how I got here. I was peacefully reading a book and sunbathing when the phone rang. Then it was sort a car out. Then it was the dash across the North Sea. Then it was the confrontation, and now the long drive back. I was weary, *very weary*.

We arrived home late that night. I phoned in. "Tell Paul YoS I'll be in at thirteen hundred tomorrow afternoon."

My body needed fuel so I ate, but tasted nothing. I showered, then crashed out.

"Phone Ray Tech," said Paul YoS when I walked in.

"Meet me on the secure line," said Ray.

"Some major players from Belfast have been spotted in Portadown. Operators and members of The Troop are seeping in and they need immediate comms. How are you fixed?"

"I'm on my way." It was the last thing I wanted!

"There's an existing antenna on the mast," said Mick. "All we have to do is connect the equipment."

"How long has the antenna been up?"

"I don't know."

"I'll make up a spare, just in case. When are we leaving?"

"When you're ready."

We tossed full mags, weapons and smoke canisters into a holdall, booked out and set off.

"We're being chaperoned on this one," said Ray. "Too risky to go it alone."

"Hello zero this is seven."

"Go ahead seven."

"We're at junction ten," I told them.

"They are at junction ten," said control.

We heard two bursts of squelch from unseen faces sat in a car somewhere.

We slipped off the M1 and onto the M12 which would lead us onto the A3 to Portadown.

"We should have been picked up by now, Ray."

"What do you reckon?"

"We'll go to just outside Portadown. If we haven't been picked up by then, we'll go back."

"Got them," came from the radio. A car parked behind us pulled out. We would be travelling through the centre of town and it would be busy. "Close your window Ray," I said, "So our Brit accents can't be overheard."

122

We stopped at a pedestrian crossing and a powerfully built man crossed. He stared into the car, too long. We were tense and drawing attention. I squeezed the pistol grip under my jacket. Felt a little bit more secure.

"You wouldn't believe what has happened to me in the last two days," I said to Ray, trying to make us both relax and look part of the scene. The big man cleared the crossing and we drove on.

"Lost them," came over the radio. We tensed and I squeezed the pistol grip a little tighter. Was it the front car that had lost us or the rear car? It didn't matter. Ten seconds later we heard, "Got them."

We parked outside the police station and waited.

"That car that pulled out behind us earlier has just gone by," said Ray. "It must be our tail." We were never sure, even to this day. We showed our IDs, then drove in. Mick and I lugged the kit from the boot into the shed at the bottom of the mast. I watched Mick connect up and left him to it. My thoughts drifted to myself. Things were catching up on me. Noises were startling me and I was becoming jumpy. The last thing I wanted was to rig this tower. I swallowed another bitter pill. The bitter pills were getting bigger, becoming more difficult to swallow as time went by. The pills didn't feel normal, but I could live with them, somehow. I gulped several times, dislodged the pill and down it sank. The bitter pill didn't have far to go as my chest was now half full. The pill left a glacial path in its wake. I monitored its movements, all the way. The pill was an individual when it started its journey, but was absorbed by the bigger one in my chest when it arrived. I'd never felt anything like it before, and the fact that it was growing worried me. I would have to have it X-ray'd.

I watched the needle on the test meter and didn't need Mick to tell me it was OK, but he did.

"Lets get outta here," he said.

We packed up and radio-ed in. "Hello zero, this is seven. We are finished."

"You are finished at your location."

Two bursts of squelch.

"Wait until the cars are in position," they said.

We sat in the car with the engine running and a policeman at the gate, waiting for the nod.

"Seven, this is zero. Leave your location now."

I nodded, the gates opened. Our chaperones picked us up, babysat us until we were clear, then left.

I felt like shit, drained of every single ounce of energy I possessed. When I got home, I couldn't even sustain a conversation. It was food and shower. Then scrub my teeth and my tongue to get rid of the yellow fur that was building up. I was smoking too much. I stared in the mirror at my tired face with the etch lines engraved in it. My tour was catching up on me.

"Eight months to push," I said aloud and winked at my reflection. "You can do it."

9

HOSPITAL VISIT

Chris was back off leave and we were now at South det installing an intercom system. There had been no night operations for a while and there were none in the foreseeable future. We got on with the intercom installation and relaxed, relishing something more technical than rigging. We had to install an intercom in every room. However, we had to be selective about where we worked due to other ongoing night operations. You could tell the type of person who lived in the room when you entered. Technicians had tools, screwdrivers and circuit diagrams scattered about their room. Members of The Troop had an array of weapons and maps. Late one afternoon I entered a room that I thought would be empty, but it wasn't. He lay there in bed and the floor told the story. I imagined him coming in completely spent, dragging his depleted body across the room to his pit. His arms must have ached from endlessly carrying his rifle and it was the first thing he'd discarded. It seemed to be alive, somehow having drawn energy from his body. It now lay on the floor, forlorn and crying for hugs. It was lonely, in solitude and out of favour. Next came his Bergen, still fully laden and all straps fastened. It lay there like an upturned turtle, its black truncheon peering from beneath. Two feet beyond his Bergen was his webbing. The heap of webbing lay dormant, its pistol still holstered. The trail continued and consisted of little blobs of cast-offs as he dropped something, walked a few more paces, dropped something else. *His pit* was his quest, the only thought in his mind. Combat jacket, complete with mud stains, shirt, complete with sweat stains. The tee shirt was next. One after another in a line. The final pile was next to his pit where, exhausted, he'd plopped onto the bed and removed them. There was a heap of dragged-off trousers, socks and shreddies. Next to the heap sat his muddy boots with thick, long, dirt-speckled laces. They reminded me of earth worms surfacing. He lay on his stomach, one arm outstretched across the pillow and his hand hanging limply over the end, comatosed and out for the count. I crept out and went for a coffee.

A large shining stainless steel water heater, constantly on the boil, stood on the draining board of the sink. Beside the heater stood boxes and jars that contained coffee, tea and sugar. They lay open and invited you to use them. A water pipe was fastened to the wall behind the sink and the pipe ran parallel to it. Three short chains were fastened to the pipe and from the chains hung three spoon handles. Sam, the detachment Technician, was also there.

"Sam, what's with these chains?" He looked around secretively, then said, "Every time the boss came for a brew there would be no plastic spoons, and it really got up his nose. He used to throw the lack of spoons into every conversation, and ask the lads to leave them there. He even brought it up at the monthly meetings." He looked around again, then continued. "One morning he put out a box of one hundred spoons, and they'd disappeared by lunchtime." He laughed before continuing, and looked around again. "The lads probably wouldn't have bothered, but he was making such a big issue of it, they smelt a victim. In the end the boss got Spanners to bolt spoons onto those chains, and then bolt the chains around those pipes," he said pointing. "Some of the lads sneaked out in the early hours and cut the ladles off the spoons. Next time you see the boss, look what's sticking out of his top pocket. He always carries his own spoon now."

We talked for a while longer, then it was time to go. On the way home I reminded Chris about tomorrow,

"We'll be around camp all day," I said. "It's Jean's hospital visit."

Jean was looking after Anna-Lisa when I got home because Belinda had got a job and was working late. I picked Anna-Lisa up, whizzed her around and made her giggle. Jean grabbed the opportunity and disappeared into the kitchen. I took Anna-Lisa upstairs, washed her and put her pyjamas on, then went back down. Anna-Lisa was always on her best behaviour when in her pyjamas and she would sit there very still and say nothing. We watched tele and ate while discussing tomorrow, then it was Anna-Lisa's bedtime.

"It's seven o' clock Anna," I said, leaning towards her.

She froze, pretended she hadn't heard and tried to become invisible. I stood up, walked over and stood between her and the tele.

"Come on Anna."

"Oh Granddad, do I have to?" I knelt down, put my back towards her and said, "Piggy back time."

"Oh all right then," she said, dragging herself off the settee.

Anna-Lisa didn't totally dislike going to bed because when she was tucked in I would read her a story. When I read to her I had different voices for different characters and threw in animal sounds as well. Tonight's story was about a lion so there were lots of roars. She cuddled beneath the sheets and drew them up to her chin when the lion roared. She would move her feet up and down and her eyes would become big and wide. I wasn't sure if she would sleep after some of the stories because she became so excited.

Belinda had a job at a local nursing home and when she was on a late shift I'd pick her up. Some nights I'd do it by car and some nights I'd be on foot. I would park in different places and wait at different points so as not to create a pattern. This particular night I drove into work, picked up my Browning, then parked close to the nursing home and waited. The door opened and she jumped in.

"Hi Dad," she said, giving me a peck on the cheek. "I phoned the girls at my last nursing home today and guess what?"

"What?"

"They've had a whip round for me and bought me a farewell present."

"That's really great. What is it?"

"It's a hand-painted flower vase and they were really worried that it would get broken in the post. Anyway, one of them has got a friend who is a carpet salesman and he comes over on a regular basis, and he said he'd drop it off at the guardroom. Could you pick it up for me?"

"Sure. When does it arrive?"

"Thursday."

"Remind me on Friday and I'll pop in."

"This is Colin," said Paul YoS the following morning. "He's a Royal Signals captain and he's been posted in to take over the admin side."

"What does your job entail, Jack?" Colin asked.

I gave him a brief outline. "Rigging, intercoms and phones," I told him, while wondering what Paul was going to do now apart from sit on his fat arse. He never went out, never made a decision, and always asked his Pronto about anything technical which he was supposed to be an expert at. Roy had once told me he had stopped answering Paul's questions and left him to it. He said he'd messed up so much that he'd had to start giving him answers again for the sake of the lads.

"Catch you later Colin," I said and headed for my office.

"Good morning Brian," I said to the back of the open news-paper. He lowered it slowly and his face appeared with a big grin on it.

"I've been dicked to organize a mess dinner for the senior NCOs and the officers in our mess," he said. I started laughing and said, "You've been on covert operations for eleven years, you won't have a clue on how to organize a mess dinner."

"Well, I'm only taking names at the moment. Are you interested?"

"Put me down as a definite for two," I told him.

"Good morning Jack, good morning Brian," said Chris as he walked in. He was always a chirpy bastard.

"What's on at the ranges this Saturday Brian?" he asked. The newspaper lowered again. "There will be two competitions, a target shoot and a balloon shoot, and there'll be a kitty." The news-paper made a crackling noise as he shook it. He jerked the paper up and hid behind it once again and said from behind it, "Now fuck off and stop bothering me."

"Did I say something wrong?" asked Chris.

"No. You're just too fucking chirpy in the mornings," said Brian, shaking the newspaper and remaining behind it.

"What are we doing today, Jack?" asked Chris.

"I've got a load of paperwork to sort out this morning. You can do what you like. After lunch Jean and I will come back and pick you up, then we'll drop her off at the hospital," I told him. "Then we will come back here and wait for her to call. Are you all right with that?"

"Sure. Sounds fine," he said, looking bored with what the morning contained for him.

I went through the procedures with Jean again, just to be sure.

"Have you got your book?" I asked.

"Yes," she said, gulping.

"Where is it?"

"In my handbag." I checked it and made sure her fags and lighter were there as well.

"This is going to be the most difficult day of your life," I told her. She looked all concerned and asked, "Why?"

"Trying not to talk for three hours is impossible." She smiled, slapped my arm and relaxed a little.

Jean had to wait in the car while I went into HQ. Chris was waiting in the ops room with the holdall and had already booked us out. We got in the car and I did a radio check, then we were off.

Everything seemed calm and normal as I drove around the car park and stopped at the steps leading into the hospital. Nurses walked back and forth and no silent cars with occupants lingered. Jean climbed out, then leaned in and kissed my cheek, like any normal couple,

"I'll give you a ring when I've finished," she said.

We drove back and sat in the office, waiting for her call.

"I can't believe I've already been here four months," said Chris. "I'm away in two."

"We're going to have some piss up that night," I said, winking at him. I was going to miss him when he went. He'd been round for dinner a couple of times and had become a friend of the family. He was a good mate, a pleasure to be with and very professional.

Ring, Ring. Chris looked up as I lifted the receiver, then he watched me. It was Jean.

"Can you pick me up on the corner?" she said.

"Sure, see you soon," I said, looking at Chris and nodding towards the door.

Jean was on the corner with her arms folded, looking towards the main road. We drove down the cul-de-sac and as we drew level with her she couldn't resist letting on. She raised her little finger, wiggled it a couple of times, then looked away. We drove past her looking straight ahead, circled the car park and observed. Everything seemed normal. I waited until we'd left the hospital grounds and were on the main road before asking, "How did it go?"

"Fine," she said. "I was a little concerned when they called my name out in the waiting room. It sounded so English after all the previous names, and everybody turned and stared when I stood up. I had to wait ages to use the phone. Somebody always seemed to be near by. The check up was OK and I should get the result in about three weeks."

She was all bubbly and bright now the appointment was behind her, and asked, "Since this is our last Christmas, what about us having a party?"

"Great idea," I said.

"I won't be here for that," said Chris, all mournful.

"I wish your posting would come in," she said to me. "It should have been here by now."

We fixed a date for the party when we got back and Jean wasted no time. She was on the phone for the next hour phoning friends. Belinda and Anna-Lisa came home laden with shopping.

"Darrrd," said Belinda. Here it comes, I thought.

"Wharrrt?"

"Are you going out for a drink this Friday?"

"Maybe," I teased.

"Well I haven't been out for ages," she said with a little pout on her face. "And I thought you might want to buy your daughter a drink."

"I'll be having a drink in The Unit bar, then going down the strip for a couple. We could meet at the guardroom at seven if that's OK?"

"Great. Oh my present from the girls should have arrived today. Can you call in the guardroom tomorrow and see if it's there?" she asked, giving me a hug.

The guards were always busy first thing in the morning, so I went into work first to pick up Chris. We were at South det today and on the way out I checked for the present.

"Has anything been left for me?" I asked giving my name.

"Oh, it's you is it?" said the corporal, and started smiling. "This carpet salesman pulled up at the guardroom yesterday and asked if he could leave a parcel for you. We checked the list so we could give you a ring, but you weren't listed." Oops! I'd forgotten that we were self-administered. Only the Unit had access to our files.

"So what happened?" I asked.

"Well," he said, smiling even more, "what would you do if someone rolled up and wanted to leave a brown paper parcel for someone that didn't exist? First we asked him to open the parcel. Then we made him unload all his carpets and went through his car like a fine toothcomb. If you want your parcel you'll have to go to the left luggage store." Chris roared when I told him.

We had a choice of jobs at South now. The old tower had become severely overloaded and a new one had been built. If it was a nice day we could work on the tower or, if it was a bad one, we could work inside on the intercom. Today was nice so we rigged, and relaxed. We relished being in a safe zone not having constantly to take precautions. We shouted to each other while running up and down the tower. Attached antennae, raised cables and enjoyed the day. It was late afternoon when I shouted down, "Chris, are you going into the bar tonight?"

"Is the Pope a Catholic?"

"Let's call it a day then."

We were on our second drink when Wayne Tech came over with an enormous grin on his face. "Remember when we talked about jump-starting a wagon with one jump lead and Brad said it couldn't be done?'

"Yeah," I said.

"Well I parked two cars close together just like you said and put a duff battery in one of them. Then I connected a black cable to an earth on one car. Ran the cable under the car and out under the boot and connected it to the earth of the other car. Then," he said gleefully, "I covered the cable with white chippings and gave Brad a shout. 'Try and start that car,' I said to Brad. The battery made a half-hearted attempt to start the engine, then it died. I grabbed a jump lead," he said, demonstrating by holding his hands apart with the fingers partly clenched as though he had the jump lead in his hands. His hands turned over as though he was connecting the jump lead to the battery and at the same time he said, "I connected the jump lead to the positive terminals of the batteries and said to Brad, 'Try that'." Wayne stepped back to give himself more space, then threw his arms up into the air and at the same time said, "The engine roared into life and you should have seen Brad's face. He was totally gobsmacked and just stood there scratching his head. This was on Tuesday," continued Wayne. "You know how Brad likes to prove everything. Well he spent the next three days on his computer trying to work it out, and this morning he comes up to me and says, 'You must have been very lucky. The cars must have had flat tyres and somehow they must have been just the right distance apart to produce capacitance'." Brad had to find an answer to everything but that was total bullshit, and who should walk in at that minute but Brad.

"What's it like having your wire pulled," shouted Wayne.

"What's it like having a jump with only one leg?" I followed. He got so much shit that night, and for the next few days, you had to feel sorry for him. Friday night had kicked off *again*! It was getting close to seven, so I said, "Got to go lads. I'm meeting my daughter and taking her down the strip for a drink. See you later."

I met Belinda and we went down to Three Nine Brigade's bar. Word had got around how gorgeous Belinda was, and I wasn't in the least bit surprised when the lads walked in. They crowded around us, chatted and laughed with Belinda, and tried to make their presence felt. Rob was already in there with his lads, winding down after a hard week. He kept looking over at Belinda and she at him. She leaned over and asked, "Who's that gorgeous hunk over there Dad?"

"Rob from Seven. Shall I drag him over?"

"Hmm!" was all she said.

He passed us on his way to the bar and nodded to me, flicked his eyes at Belinda and then carried on. Everybody in the crowd sensed the huge chemical and physical reaction they'd generated between them. The lads who had been trying to chat her up melted away and fell silent; they realized their cause was now in vain. Rob took some drinks over to his lads, then came back for the one he'd left on the bar. Just as he was passing I said, "Rob, how you doin'?" He stopped and joined us. "Rob, this is Belinda," I said. They shook hands and sparks flew. They were still chatting away an hour later when I said I'd had enough.

"I'm going home Belinda. Are you coming?"

"It's a bit early Dad. I think I'll stay a bit longer."

"Fine. Make sure she gets a taxi will you, Rob."

"Sure."

"Catch you later Belinda."

"OK, Dad. Thanks for bringing me out," she said, leaning over and pecking me on the cheek.

I told Jean what had happened when I got home and you could see her putting two and two together, and hopefully making four.

Belinda was spooning egg into Anna-Lisa's mouth when I strolled into the kitchen.

"Good morning Anna-Lisa," I said.

"Good morning Grandad," she said with bits of egg falling out of her mouth. Belinda gave me a tight-lipped 'look what you've done' smile, so I leaned over and hugged her.

"Have a good night last night?" I asked.

"Yes. Rob walked me to the guardroom and got me a taxi."

"Fancy Rob walking you to the guardroom. I'd never have guessed." She smiled and carried on spooning.

"Darrrd?" Something's coming I thought.

"Wharrrt?"

"Are you going out tonight?"

"I don't think we've got anything planned. Why?"

"Rob's asked me out, and I wondered if you would mind babysitting?"

"It's fine by me, but check with your Mum," I said.

We were packed in the kitchen, which was normal for Saturday morning. We discussed the week's and Friday night's events, throwing banter at each other and generally having a good time. I checked the time and said, "Isn't it about time we were going, lads?"

The cars were parked outside and as soon as a driver jumped into a car the passenger seats would fill. It was disorganized organization going to the ranges, but it worked. Brian had got it all set up when we arrived and he now stood before us outlining the morning in his usual short sharp sentences.

"There will be two individual shoots," he began. "I'll call you forward for the first shoot. It will be individual and timed. The second will be a fast draw eliminator. There are practice stands, so if you would like to wander around, I'll call you forward when I'm ready. Thank you." We began to disperse then he shouted. "Rigger, where are you going?" I couldn't help but laugh. Everybody else did.

I was stood on the fifty-metre line listening once again to Brian who was enjoying himself. He was smiling like hell and looking straight at me.

"When you hear my whistle run to the first box and kneel down behind it. Three targets will rise in front of you and I want a double tap [two shots] on each. The targets will fall after fifteen seconds. Wait until they come up again and then run to the second box and kneel behind it. I want a double tap on each target again. The same procedure applies to the third exposure." He was grinning, loving every minute. He really enjoyed setting me up.

I dashed to the first box when he blew the whistle. I knelt down behind it and double-tapped the first two targets. I was slow off the mark and the third target was on its way down before I'd aimed. I snatched the trigger in my haste, loosed off two rounds and knew I'd missed, then waited. The targets came up again, so I dashed to the second box, skidded in on one knee and double-tapped. Twelve rounds were gone and my magazine was empty.

I pressed the magazine release button and the magazine squirted into my hand. I slipped the empty magazine into the magazine holder on my belt, withdrew a full one and inserted it in the pistol grip, then tapped it with the heel of my hand to make sure it was home. There was no need to re-cock the pistol. The working parts were still to the rear from the previous shot. The targets came up for the last time and I dashed over. Sweat was pouring down my face, not because of the amount of physical exercise, but because of the urgency of it. I saw two holes appear on each target this time and I stood up feeling better. The score would definitely not win the shoot, but it was reasonable. I ejected the magazine out of the pistol, cocked the pistol three times, then withdrew the other magazine from its holder. I held all three up for inspection and pointed them backwards. Brian looked over my shoulder, checked them, then slapped my back for confirmation and said, "Gun clear."

"You bastard Brian," I said.

"Who? Me?" he said, poking his finger in his chest, leaning back slightly and grinning all over his face. I brushed paste over the holes and Brian followed, patching up and counting.

"Twelve," he shouted so that everybody watching could hear. Then, "crap," he said and burst out laughing. Brian pushed me towards the smiling crowd and continued to entertain them. "Come on junior rigger, you're next."

Chris, the gangly youth, was still amazing me with his abilities and his professionalism. He stood there poised, waiting for the whistle, then ran over on its command and knelt behind the box. His actions were smooth and fluid as he lined up, double-tapped, scanned right and double-tapped again. He was fast, efficient and graceful all at the same time, and went through the mag change with time to spare. After the last exposure he rose purposefully but without urgency. He cleared his weapon, pasted up the targets and came over.

"How'd you do Chris?"

"Seventeen," he said with all the calm in the world, shrugging his shoulders.

The shoot was going to take a long time and to keep us occupied

Brian had set up another twenty-metre range for standard practice. Rob was converting brass to scrap when we got there and came over when he'd finished. He was a little tense and the lads around him sensed it. They went quiet as he approached me and watched.

"Have a good night Rob?" I asked. He still wasn't sure how the father of the girl he took out last night would react, so I broke the ice.

"Off for a chinkie tonight?" I asked him. He relaxed and smiled and the silence around us evaporated.

"Yeah," he said. "It's ages since our unit has had a night out, so we're off for a meal tonight. Should be good." He paused, wondering what to say next, then said, "Simon Stores has brought his Magnum down. Have you ever fired one?"

"No I haven't."

"Have a go; it's a beast. I'm off to the other range. Catch you later."

The Magnum was generating a lot of interest and you had to queue up to fire it. Chris and I had a go and both came to the same conclusion. It was heavy to handle. It was difficult to hold in the firing position for any length of time and difficult to hit the target with. Dirty Harry could keep it.

We gathered at the competition range and waited for Brian to announce the winner of the first shoot. He could have come over then, but made us wait by pretending to add up the scores, which he already knew. That man should have been in show biz.

"The winner is," he said, then paused, looked at our anxious faces and smiled, "The winners are," he began again, "Chris Rigger and John Tech, with a score of seventeen. There's thirty-four quid in the kitty. Come over here and collect it," he said, holding up his knitted hat.

We calmed and waited for Brian again. "It will be a fast draw eliminator shoot," he continued. "Your names are in that box," he said, pointing to a box on a table. "They will be drawn out in threes. You will stand on the thirty-metre mark with your pistols holstered and wait for my whistle. There will be four balloons pinned to each target and the first person to pop them all will go through to the next round. Give me your one pounds as you come up. Are there any questions?"

Stu Clerk had been wandering around the office all week with an empty weapon, practising fast draws in the hope that he might win today. It had got that bad that the lads in the offices had begun to whistle the theme tune from 'A Fist Full Of Dollars' whenever he entered their room. Stu was standing on the firing line with Alan Clerk and Tony Bleep and I began to whistle. It was picked up by the person next to me and had a knock-on effect. There were now forty soldiers whistling the theme tune and Brian couldn't blow the whistle for laughing. He kept putting the whistle to his mouth, bursting out laughing then pulling it away. He walked over to us, still laughing. Threw his arms open and said, "You're not taking this serious are you?" Once again he stole the show. He walked back, stood to the left of the firing line and said, "Wait for my whistle."

Stu drew first and took out the four balloons without dropping a shot. He was through to the next round. What he didn't know was that in six weeks' time he would pay for the most expensive carpet in his life, four hundred pounds a square foot. Trevor Pronto, myself and Rob Seven were next. We all wanted to win, but I suspected Rob more than us. If he lost I would most certainly tell Belinda and she would most certainly mention it to him. I sensed him staring at me while we were standing on the firing line. I turned and he smiled at me. I smiled back. I looked to the front, got my head together and waited.

Whistle-draw-shoot. It was all over in seconds and it was close. We waited for the verdict. "Rob's the winner," proclaimed Brian.

Rob slapped me on the back and said, "Tough shit eh!"

"Didn't want to show you up with an old bastard like me winning. I gave it you."

"Well thanks for that," he said, knowing full well I'd bust a gut to try and win.

We went through the preliminary rounds, the semi-final and on to the final. Stu Clerk, Rob Seven and John Tech were in with a chance. They wandered off to find space and get their heads together. It was going to be tight and Brian knew it. Brian had asked Chris and I to act as additional judges and we now stood behind the firing line waiting for the shooters. They came over, stood before the targets and waited. Brian lifted the whistle to his mouth and looked at Chris and me. We nodded.

There was silence everywhere, tension and excitement. The only moving things were the balloons. They were tethered to their targets and they bobbed up and down full of life, trying to release themselves and escape the coming death. It must have taken three or four seconds for them to draw their weapons and shoot, but it seemed like one second expanded. They loosed off their rounds so quickly it was as thought one shot had been fired, and the sound stretched. A deathly silence and a total stillness fell upon us, and that unreal feeling entered me again. It felt like Groundhog Day where we were back at the beginning again. The only thing that had changed since just before the shoot were the balloons. They hung in tatters. They had been full, round, vibrant, bouncy, smiling, colourful and gay. They now hung lifeless and reminded me of Del and Dave.

One minute here – the next minute! A feeling of deep sorrow passed through me and another bitter pill formed. I gulped and swallowed.

The firing party was set in stone and remained there, perfectly still, waiting for the command to unload. I also remained still, and so did Chris and Brian. It had all happened so fast, it was difficult to take in. I searched my memory and ran the pictures through again. The whistle! The elongated shot! The balloons bursting! Then – the conclusion. Brian stepped forward and his movement broke the stillness, triggering more movement.

"Unload," he shouted.

The silence disintegrated and a buzz of conversation rose from the spectators. Weapons were cocked several times to ensure the chambers were empty, then held up for inspection. We took one person each, peered into their chamber and declared, "Gun clear."

The three of us went into a huddle and Brian asked, "Who do you reckon, Chris?"

"It was close, but I thought it was Rob."

"What about you, Jack?"

I said one word. "John."

Conversation died as Brian made his way over to the crowd and they waited expectantly. He stood in front of them and guess what? He hung it out.

"Hurry up Brian, I want to go home," somebody shouted. He looked up, not in the least bit affected, paused for a few more seconds, then said, "John."

10

CHRIS'S FAREWELL

Chris and I had spent the last few days pottering around HQ moving intercoms and telephones due to office relocation. We were putting the finishing touches to the moves when a massive cheer echoed down the corridor from the direction of the control room.

"Must be something good," said Chris, with a puzzled look on his face.

"Well let's find out," I said.

We weren't the only nosey parkers. People peered out of office doors as we walked by they seemed to be sucked out to tag along behind as we made our way down. The crowd and the chatter increased as we neared the control room and we finished up a merry throng bumbling along to see what was what. It made me feel like the Pied Piper without the flute.

I stood in the doorway of the ops room with each arm outstretched, hands pressing against the doorframe to prevent everyone from bursting in. The throng pushed up behind, halted and fell silent. It was obvious we wouldn't disturb anything by going in as the two Bleeps were jubilant, sitting back in their chairs with their feet resting on their desks. I dropped my hands and they slapped heads that had been pushed under my arms to peer in. Nosey bastards, I thought. They followed silently, shuffling around the control room trying to find space where they could park themselves so that they see and hear. The two Bleeps looked at each other with big grins on their faces and waited.

"What was the cheering for, Tony?" asked one of the nosey parkers.

"We've just been listening in to an operation taking place with regards to the IRA. They were trying to assassinate a delivery driver who was changing a flat tyre."

"How'd it go?" asked an over-eager voice.

"It didn't go exactly to plan, but worked out well in the end," said John Bleep. He left it at that and sat back.

"Well go on," somebody pushed him.

"Well," he said, shuffling his bum and making himself more comfortable. "We'd been listening in for about half an hour when we heard, 'They're here'. The next thing we hear is 'They've gone. They just slowed down, looked at him and drove off'."

"You're joking," came a voice from the back of the room.

The tension that had built up in the room eased a little as a ripple of laughter washed around.

"The next message we got was 'Car approaching,' then 'Wrong car,' then, '*Fire*'. Boy, did we sit up! The shooting started before he'd let go of the transmit button and all we heard was a flood of shots. We think that the IRA had another car parked down the road that they were going to use as a getaway car, and that they had driven past, and come back in the getaway car. Course, when this other car appeared it threw us," he said, as though he was there taking part. "It was only when they opened up we knew who they were. Bullets were flying all around, then all hell broke loose."

The Troop had poured rounds into the car and ripped it and its occupants to shreds. My tour had seemed so one-sided until now and it was good to get one back. I thought about Del and Dave. I thought about the sheer frustration of having to soldier on while your mates were picked off. It's a bitter pill. I rubbed my chest again and the cold chunk in there was now enormous. I'd have to get it X-rayed.

People filtered out and disappeared back to their offices, laughing and excited, wanting to tell others. Chris looked at me and said, "What now, boss?" I thought about it, and I didn't feel like doing any more work today. "Office," I said.

Because of the location of our office, Brian hadn't heard a thing, so we told him.

"They'll have some piss-up tonight," he said. It started him reminiscing about the old days at North Det.

"We used to have some wild piss-ups," he began. "The bar windows had been broken that often that in the end we installed removable ones. We'd try to think of different ways to enter the bar on the piss-ups, and one night somebody poured petrol across the entrance and lit the petrol. The only way in was through the flames or it was no beer. We all made it. It reminded me of Guy Fawkes Night, but I've never been to a bonfire like that one. You know Tom Seven?" he asked. Tom had earned the Queen's Gallantry Medal not once but twice. He'd left the British army on a couple of occasions to work in some African state but had been readily accepted back because of his experience.

"Yeah," I nodded.

"Well, we had this huge bonfire going in the compound. Music was pouring out of the bar and we were all stood around eating and drinking and generally having a good time. Tom's a mad bastard," said Brian, lowering his head down to his chest and shaking it. He raised it and said, "There we were enjoying ourselves when Tom comes running up and throws a jerry can full of petrol on to the fire."

"What!" exclaimed Chris, standing up and looking amazed, with his lower jaw drooping. "What did you do?"

"Fucking run," said Brian. "We were peering around the corners of buildings and watching as this jerry can swelled up when I decided to go and get a rifle. I lined up on the can," he said, lifting his arms up as though aiming a rifle. "BOOM!" he shouted, throwing himself back in his chair as though it was the recoil of the rifle and bursting out laughing. "I nearly shit myself as this huge great jet of flame shot towards me. WHOOSH! I thought I was a goner," he said, throwing his arms back. "Luckily it didn't reach me. The camp guard surrounded the place because they thought we were under attack. In the end we had to phone the guardroom and tell them everything was OK." The ambush had invoked a lot of old memories for Brian and they came flooding out. His eyes were sparkling and he continued, "It was that mad bastard Tom that started most of it. I was stood at the bar one night, quietly drinking my beer when this body came through the ceiling and landed on my shoulders. One minute I was having a quiet beer and the next I was covered in plaster with a body on top of me. Tom had crept into the attic, worked out where I was and jumped through the ceiling on top of me. We used to have this big over-head fan," he said, lowering his head again and putting it in his hands. He shook his head and looked up, "We used to throw full cans of beer into the fan and the fan used to kick them out in a big way if it caught them right. Somebody would shout '*can*' and we'd all go rigid, and stand there waiting," he said, standing up and stiff-ening his body while looking straight ahead. "The can would go up into the fan and it would be hurtled out. You could see it coming towards you sometimes," he said, pointing his head forward slightly but remaining perfectly still. "But you didn't dare move or it was a round of drinks." He flinched his head slightly as though a can was coming towards him, then continued. "The fan would sometimes slice into the can and beer used to shower every-where. One guy had to have stitches," he said, drawing his finger across his forehead. His encounters were rolling out of him and he sat down before continuing. "One of the funniest things was when two of us went to search a known IRA house. We went in through the skylight and the guy I was with put his foot through the ceiling. They would have known that someone had been in, so we decided to make it look like a robbery. After we'd searched the place we looked round for something to nick. The only thing of any value was the fridge. So we dragged this fridge across a field, then hid in a hedge and radioed for a pick-up. You should have seen the look on the driver's face." Tears were rolling down Brian's face from laughing and we had to wait for him. "The look on the driver's face," he began again, "when we threw this fridge on the back seat. The driver said, 'What the fuck's that?' 'A fucking fridge, what does it look like?' I told him. When we got back we put the fridge in the bar and filled it with beer; I think it's still there. Every time I went into the bar and saw it I'd start laughing."

The phone rang and it was for me. Nick Chief (clerk) was on

the other end and he told me my posting had come through. I was off to Germany for my last two-year tour, and then it was back to good old Blighty for six months' resettlement. Being called Mister sounded good again. Boy, was I smiling when I put the phone down!

"Good news?" asked Chris.

"Brilliant news," I told him. "My posting's in and I'm off to Germany. Well, they're not going to get anything else out of me this afternoon. So I'm off home to tell Jean. See you in the morning."

Everything was falling into place. Two months to Christmas and what a wing ding that was going to be. A couple of months run down the other side of Christmas, then Germany. Rob, Belinda and Anna-Lisa were getting on so well that we were looking after Anna-Lisa while Rob and Belinda searched for a house in England.

Chris and I did one more rigging task together before he left. It was more surveillance equipment on the tower at Coalisland police station. I decided to do it on the Tuesday night, so we'd be in shape for Chris's farewell on the Friday. Ground support troops had been booked and the rigging kit had been checked and tested by Tuesday morning. John and Ray Tech were coming along to do the technical side and they were in the same position as us, ready to roll. We decided to knock off and meet at ten that night. As they were leaving I said, "Oh by the way, Colin and Brian are coming along."

"What's behind that?" asked Ray.

"Brian has never seen any rigging done before and wants to come along just for the ride. And Colin wants to get in on the rigging side as he has nothing to do." So much for Paul YoS putting a case forward for an officer to be posted in to help with the workload. What workload?

"OK, see you at ten," said Ray.

We met at ten, drew our weapons, booked out, did a radio check and set off. Half a mile from the police station we passed three green teams tabbing in. Once again they'd been dropped off on the outskirts as it was safer and made their own way in on foot. Two youths were walking towards us as we sat waiting for the gates to open and, after the last time, I was taking no chances. I stepped out of the car with the support weapon, knelt down and looked them in the eye. Then with sharp stabbing finger motions pointed to the pavement on the other side of the road. They got the message. The gates opened and I followed the cars in on foot.

"Leave the gates open," I told the policeman. "The foot patrols are just up the road." He stepped out onto the pavement, looked up the road, nodded and waited.

"What was all that about?" said Colin, laughing.

"Is this your first visit to Coal Island?" I asked him. Before he could reply Brian shouted me over. "Jack, look at that." Brian was looking up at the mast, so I joined him.

"The mast is leaning over," he told me.

I looked up and he was right. The top section was leaning severely to the left where we'd mounted the first camera.

"What are you going to do?" asked Colin.

"Cancel the job."

"What about the green teams?"

"They'll get an early night."

It was my job and I deemed it unsafe to climb. It was the first job where I'd refused to climb. The reason behind it was not because of terrorist activity, but for technical reasons. The green teams were over the moon and wasted no time in calling their transport back. We packed up and left after them. Colin was driving and he did his Blues Brothers thing. He squealed the tyres as he pulled away. It made me wince.

I went to see Paul YoS the next morning and told him about the problem.

"So how do we get round it?" he asked.

"Well, a stronger mast will have to be built to take the extra load."

"How do we do that?"

"It's police property and they'll have to put it out to contract. That's one for you. I don't have the time."

He wasn't happy with the situation and it showed. He pondered for a few minutes then looked up. "The light on the new mast at South isn't working. The contractors who built it will be there at eleven this morning. Can you liaise?"

145

"Sure. No problem," I said and walked out of his office, turned the corner, then BANG!

I ran back and looked into the ops room just in time to see Tony Bleep taking a Browning off Stu Clerk. Stu was stood mesmerized, in shock and looking down at the carpet. There was a hole in the carpet so I knelt down to examine it. The round had gone through the carpet and gouged a hole in the concrete floor. Smears of lead lined the hole and fragments of concrete must have been blasted everywhere.

"Anybody hurt?" I asked, standing up looking around. Nobody answered and they all seemed fine. A crowd was rapidly gathering at the door, so I pushed my way through and left them to it. I'd get the details later.

"What was the bang?" asked Chris as I walked into the office.

"Stu ND'd [negligently discharged] in the ops room."

"Anybody hurt?"

"No. I disappeared quickly. I hate paperwork."

"What's on today?" asked Chris.

"You know that new tower at South?"

"Yeah."

"Well, apparently the light's not working on the top, and we're meeting the contractors to try and sort it out. We'll be leaving at ten, so relax."

They were waiting at the foot of the tower when we arrived, two of them, a skinny one and a thick broad-set one who must have been the boss, as he did all the talking.

"Before we go any further I'll check out the light," he said, putting on his belt. He made his way up the central ladder with that easy, confident action of a man used to heights. His feet stepped on every rung on the way up while his hands gripped every other rung. His body rippled smoothly and he made his way up to the top without rest. It was bread and butter to him. I couldn't see what was happening at the top, but whatever it was it didn't take long. It's easier on the way down and he had it. Every other rung with the hands and every other rung with his feet. He came over to me whilst unclipping his belt and said, "The problem is that you've got a two twenty-volt fitting and a one ten-volt supply."

146

I was amazed at this, as he wasn't carrying any test equipment.

"How do you know that?" I asked.

"I disconnected the wires at the top and flashed them across each other," he said, moving his right hand over his left as though striking a match. "There was only a dull spark, so it must be one ten."

I couldn't believe it. He had stood on top of a mast at one hundred and fifty feet with two live wires in his hands touching them together.

"When we built the mast I knew the 220V specification for the light was wrong as we always fit one ten for safety," he said. "But I couldn't find anybody to ask. We don't fit the power supplies, but if you go and check it you'll find it's one ten." I went inside and sure enough the power supply was one ten.

"Well thanks for coming over," I said to the foreman, "and you're right, it is the wrong light fitting. Can you leave it with me and I'll sort it?" He nodded and left.

"Shall we pop in and have a chat with Bill Spanner?" asked Chris.

"Yeah, good idea," I said.

We looked around the workshop but couldn't see him.

"What about his office?" asked Chris. We walked over, peered in, but he wasn't there either. There were four or five operators and members of The Troop standing around a normal looking Sierra, so we walked over and asked them,

"Any idea where Bill is?" I asked

"Yeah he's gone for spares. What do you think of this?" said one of the crowd pointing to the Sierra. I looked at the basic two-year-old Sierra and said, "Not much."

"It cost sixty thousand pounds," he said, smiling.

We'd obviously missed something, so we gave it a closer look. We walked round it and peered inside it but we still couldn't see where sixty thousand pounds had been spent. Chris and I looked at each other and shrugged our shoulders.

"OK, what's so special?" I asked.

"This car has had its sixteen hundred engine taken out and it's been replaced with a fine-tuned three litre one. The engine torque has increased so much that the gearbox and drive shaft have been upgraded. The extra speed and weight gave cornering problems so the soft suspension has been replaced with a harder suspension. It's got armour plating and special comms." He reminded me of a used car salesman the way he ran through all the upgrades and gadgets.

"What's it like on the road?" asked Chris.

"Don't know. We only took delivery today and nobody has been out in it yet. The trials won't happen until some time next week."

Chris and I spent the next couple of days in camp. I was sorting out the rigging shack and ordering stores while Chris was doing his clearing. Clearing can be a pain. You receive two sheets of paper with all the departments listed on them and all you have to do is go to the relevant department and get their signature. It can sometimes take up to three days to clear, with visits to the troop store, squadron store, regimental store or the sports store to make sure that you are not disappearing with their kit. The library needs to be visited to make sure you're not leaving with one of their books. The dental centre needs to be visited so they can forward your documents, and the medical centre needs to be visited so that they can forward your documents and check to see if you need any jabs for your next posting. The one you don't want to go to is the NAAFI. The NAAFI ensures that any HP transactions you've taken out follow you. You see the troop sergeant, the troop officer commanding, the squadron sergeant major, the squadron officer commanding and the squadron clerk. Some of them get right up your nose with their petty little ways. It must be a contagious disease acquired by stores staff, probably brought on by them never seeing an end product, but just putting things on shelves and taking them off again. They look down their noses at you and give you a blank uninterested look and they all have that 'I'm doing you a favour' mannerism. They also talk down to you and come out with the same pat lines, which are embedded in their brain at birth:

"I'm not signing until he's signed."

"That's damaged, you'll have to pay for a new one."

"I'm just going for a coffee, you'll have to come back later."

You have to be nice or you don't get their signatures.

ASSHOLES

Friday afternoon Chris came down to the riggers' shack waving his air tickets after visiting the last one on his list, the movement clerk. All he had to do now was pick up his cases and go. We popped into the tech workshop to remind them it was Chris's farewell tonight. They hadn't forgotten and promised to be there. Stu Clerk was duty barman this month and we stood at the bar waiting for him to arrive. He came in beaming from ear to ear, so I asked the obvious.

"What are you looking so happy about?"

"I'm not really that happy, just glad it's all over," he said. "I've just bought the most expensive carpet in the world, four hundred pounds a square foot." He bent down and opened the fridge, fished out two Guinness and placed them on the bar in front of us.

"Go on then, tell us," prompted Chris.

"Remember when I N.D.'d [negligent discharge] into the floor? All they had to do was put a bit of concrete into the hole and fit a new carpet tile. I've just been on orders and fined four hundred pounds for it."

Somebody else came in and asked Stu, "How'd you get on?" It was going to be a popular question tonight so we moved away from the bar. The lads from Five and Seven came in and so did the girls from the office. Nick Chief joined us and soon the place was heaving. The bar was so packed that people even spilled into the corridor. Consequently, more people came in as they heard the buzz. I'd got my silly head on, *again*! I grabbed Nick Chief's arm and dragged him down the corridor then into his office,

"Come on Nick, lets do a streak." He hesitated for a few seconds, thought about it then said, "OK," and started to unbutton his shirt. I was standing with my hand on the door handle, totally naked, waiting for Nick to take off his shreddies when he said, "Can't do it."

"Come on Nick. You're nearly there."

"No I can't."

"You can't back out now Nick," I pressed. He hesitated, then said, "Okay, but I'm going to wear my raincoat. I'll keep it open though." He'd gone as far as he was prepared to, so I said, "All right, but you go first."

149

"Don't you dare lock the door on me when I'm in the corridor," he said suspiciously, pointing at me and laughing.

"The thought never occurred to me Nick," I said, pushing him out. We started to run down the corridor towards the bar and the people in the corridor yahoo'ed and created space for us to run into the bar. They shouted, "Streakers."

The noise was deafening when we ran into the bar and a passage opened up to the right and along the front of the bar. Nick ran down it, I followed. It was the second bar stool along that caused the problem. It was stood a little bit further out from the bar than the others were and Nick tripped over it. He nose-dived forward, fell and rolled onto his back. It was the worst possible place he could have fallen because he was now sprawled at the feet of the only two girls in the bar. He looked up at them with his raincoat wide open and grimaced. The roar in the bar turned to silence and you could have heard a pin drop. The girls looked down and one of them very casually lifted her glass to her mouth, took a sip and said, "Not bad for a skinny bastard."

Boy, did it break the ice and a huge roar ensued. I bent down, picked Nick up and helped him back to the office. All he could say was, "Don't tell my wife. She'd kill me."

An hour later people started to drift. Some went home and some of us went down to The Strip. You never think you will meet certain people again and then it happens.

"Jack," somebody shouted as I walked into The Posties bar. I turned and there was Dinger (Neild Bell, Lance Corporal). We'd rigged and worked together in different parts of the world and here we were bumping into each other again. He came over and we chatted about old times. Somebody told him about the streak earlier and he said, "That's nothing. When I [that wonderful squaddie start to a sentence] was in the Falklands I made the mistake of asking him," he said, pointing towards me and raising his voice on the 'him', "to look after my camera while I went for a game of squash, I made a bad mistake. It was a couple of months before I posted the film off for developing and the next thing I know is my missus phoning me at work. She said the photos had arrived and there were pictures of a man's dick, and, what was I doing when I was in the Falklands. It was ages before I found out who it was and this bastard," he said, pointing his finger toward me again, "had to come round to the house and tell the missus it was him. She wouldn't believe me," he said, poking his finger in his chest.

Dinger joined us on the piss and we toured the bars together. We relived the experiences we'd had together and prompted each other with 'remember when!" We drank the night away, hoping it would go on for ever, but it never does. There was sadness in our eyes as Chris and I said goodbye. We'd developed a deep bond between us; it was now going to be broken.

"You never know. We might bump into each other again," were my parting words.

We haven't.

On my way out of the bar I passed Brad. He'd got his imaginary Green Beret on again and was squaring up to the biggest guy in the bar; I couldn't help but laugh. The big guy was looking down at Brad with an amused look on his face and knew he could have just blown Brad over if Brad had stood still long enough. I grabbed his arm and said, "Come on Brad, we're going home." His nickname for me was Captain Sensible, as I nearly always knew when I'd had enough and went home.

"Oh! Captain Sensible has arrived," he slurred. "Got to go home. See you mate," he said, holding his hand out to the big guy as though they were now the best of mates. The big guy shook his hand, winked at me and walked away.

When I'm drunk I snore, and when I drink Guinness I fart a lot. Jean knew exactly how I would arrive home and I didn't disappoint her. She had the spare room waiting for me.

11

TREVOR

I was having a bad dream. Somebody was shaking me and it disturbed me. I groaned and turned over in the hope that it would go away, but it wouldn't. It seemed to take an aeon for me to realize that it wasn't a dream. Then it took a century to dredge myself from a deep sea sleep. I surfaced and moaned as the first spasm of hangover pain shot through my head. I steadied myself and tried to work out how to move without causing pain. I tensed my neck and turned stiff-necked; it didn't work. Another bolt of lightning flashed through my head, leaving coloured spots before my eyes. I paused, let the pain subside and tried again. There was no escape. My eyelids had huge clam shells attached to them and it took a super-human effort to raise them. Jean stood there,

"Phone call from work," she said.

I tried to speak but my mouth was all furred up and dried. It came out like a croak.

"What time is it?" I asked.

"Seven o'clock."

To reduce the pain, movements would have to be done one at a time, and slowly. I decided I would only move one part of my body at a time. I slithered my right leg under the quilt like an octopus tentacle, searching for the edge of the bed. It stopped halfway and waited for the left leg to catch up. They nestled together and sought comfort from each other by rubbing themselves together. I rested them and waited for the thunderstorm in my head to subside, then carried on. My legs emerged from under the quilt, slid overboard and dangled there. The cold North Sea washed around them and roused me a little more. Courage was needed for the next movement which was guarantied to cause more pain, so I paused. I put my right palm on the mattress, raised my body slightly and drew my palm towards me a couple of inches. I repeated the motion and slowly but surely my body began to rise, with pain. I thought about resting as I neared the top, but binned the idea (even though it was a good one) as I would probably have never reached the vertical position. I caught a movement in the corner of my eye as Jean left the bedroom. She knew I wouldn't go back to sleep now that I had got this far, so she was off to tell them I was on my way.

I placed both my hands on the edge of the bed and pushed up. I swayed slightly as my hands left the bed and my feet took the weight. I moved my head slowly, casting my eyes around the room and tried to locate my jeans. I honed in on a lifeless crumpled heap in the corner which had been chucked there the night before. It took three steps to reach them and once there I lowered my body by bending my knees. I looked directly ahead and tried not to tilt my head, while groping around the floor. I touched them, grabbed them and stood up. I leaned against the wall and tried to put the jeans on without looking down. After four attempts of trying to find the leg I gave up and looked down. My brain fell forward and hammered onto the inside of my forehead. I had to look up again. UGH! I clenched my teeth and leaned forward, found the left leg of the jeans and slipped my left leg into it. Going down stairs wasn't easy as every step drove a nail into my brain. I grimaced all the way.

"Did they say what it was about?" I asked.

"No, they wouldn't say anything," said Jean, holding out the phone.

Jean stood nearby and listened to my side of the conversation.

"Hello."

"What do you want me to do?"

"Send a car round."

I put my arms around Jean and caressed her to give her a feeling of security, then said, "They shot Trevor last night. He's dead. I've got to go in and sort a few things."

153

I stood looking out of the window and nothing moved outside, just another peaceful morning. I swallowed two aspirin and forced as much milk down my throat as I could without throwing up, trying to rehydrate myself for the coming task. I recognized the car as it turned the corner, grabbed my coat and went out.

Colin explained the situation to me.

"Trevor and John Tech went out last night to do that job at Coal Island where you said the mast was overloaded," he said.

I couldn't believe that, after putting in my report about the mast being overloaded, someone else had been asked to do the same job. Trevor and John were not qualified riggers; they had only attended a Safe to Climb course; my ruling should have stood. Whoever had asked them probably sat at a desk all day and was too frightened to go out himself, but only too willing to send others. The job wasn't even classed as vital or urgent!

"Somebody opened up on them with an automatic weapon," he continued. "The first burst of shots missed them and they managed to unhook their belts and make their way down. It was when they were half-way down that the second burst came and Trevor got hit. John was lucky again. They believe the shot wasn't fatal on Trevor, but it was the fall that killed him. Silence reigned for a few minutes while I gathered my thoughts, then I said, "What were the ground troops doing?"

"There weren't any," said Colin.

I was stunned.

We walked into the thick atmosphere of the office and Colin asked, "What do you need to finish the job?"

"I need to speak to John to see how far they got?" I told him.

"Ray's on his way up and he's had a word with John. He'll fill you in with the details," said Colin.

Ray and Frank Tech walked in, closely followed by Pete Tech, who had only recently arrived.

"Ray, how much work needs to be done to finish the job?" I asked Ray.

"John said all the kit had been mounted at the top, the cables had been terminated, and all that was left to do was to fasten the cables to the leg of the mast."

They'd probably been up the mast for just over three hours. Another fifteen minutes and they'd have finished. Life could be a shit sometimes!

"OK," said Colin. "We go to Coal Island, finish the job, then Jack and I will go to Dungannon police station to collect Trevor's personal effects. We'll take two cars and make our own ways back."

Before anybody could move I stepped forward and grabbed everyone's attention. "I want this to be totally professional," I began. "We're not going *in*, or *out*, with our tail between our legs. We'll drive in slowly, and we'll exit slowly. I do not want to hear the squeal of tyres." I emphasized each point and modulated my voice for impact, then looked everybody in the eye for confirmation.

"What are we going to do about this?" said Ray, pushing his finger into Pete's chest. Pete seemed larger than normal, so I stepped forward and prodded him. He was wearing a bullet-proof vest beneath his jumper and the problem was he didn't blend in any more. Anyone looking at him would sense there was something different about him and it would start them thinking. There was fear in his eyes and he couldn't hold eye contact with me. He became all fidgety, bowed his head and gazed at the floor. I could tell him to take the vest off, but what state was his mind in? The job didn't present any great danger. It was straight in and straight out.

"Let's go," I said.

Green teams had been called in after the shooting to search the area and they were just leaving the police station as we arrived. A policeman leaned nonchalantly on the open gates and pushed himself up and walked over to us, checked our IDs and waved us in. He'd had a busy day.

The lean at the top of the mast was definitely worse than the last time I'd seen it. The additional equipment that had been erected was having an effect and I pondered. Trevor and John had been up there together and it supported them. There would only be me this time! In normal circumstances I would have still said no, but the situation had changed. I opened the boot of the car and reached in, pulled my belt out and put it on. A man dressed in civvies who had been stood at the foot of the mast when we arrived came over to me and introduced himself.

"C.I.D.," he said, flashing his warrant card. "Are you going to climb the mast?" he asked.

"Yes. Is there a problem?"

"No, but I've walked the area and I think the firing came from a pub car park up the road. Could you take some shots of the surrounding area from the top of the mast for me?" he asked, offering me a camera. I hung the camera around my neck and walked over to the mast. At the foot of the mast lay a pool of Trevor's congealed blood. It reminded me of a blob of off-coloured tarmac, which had been literally dropped on the floor while still warm, and allowed to run out to find it's own level before it solidified. The blob's edges were perfectly round and they jutted out slightly to form a small overhang. The small overhang was caused by the cold concrete cooling the bottom of the blob first, while the top still flowed outwards. It wasn't just the shape that made it look like tarmac but also the colour. Gone was the bright bubbly redness of life. The blackness of death had crept in and given it an appearance of past life. I looked up and around the yard. People stood in small groups with their heads bowed and they whispered to one another, as one does in this situation.

"Can somebody clean this up?" I shouted to no one in particular. Somebody got a bucket of water and swilled the congealed blood down a drain. Goodbye Trevor.

I looked up at the mast and I could see that the cables were already zip-tied to the top twenty feet of the mast. Another five minutes was all it would have taken for them to have finished!

"Ray," I shouted across the yard. He came over. "Can you zip the cables while I take some shots from the top of the mast?" He nodded and put his belt on.

I was off up the mast at a sure and steady pace, no scurrying or rushing, just steady and professional. I leaned back in my belt at the top of the mast and looked around, daring anybody to take a shot at me. I raised the camera to my eye and started snapping from the left and panned round to the right. After development, he would be able to lay the snaps side by side, which would give him a panoramic view. I paused and lowered the camera as the pub car park came into view and I looked at it. An oval antenna between myself and the car park caught my eye. There was a hole in the antenna where a round had passed through. There was also another hole on the other side of the oval element. I lowered myself, gazed through the two holes and lined them up. The C.I.D. detective had been right, the two holes lined up directly on the pub car park. I was too close to the mast to get a good shot through the two holes with the camera so I unclipped my belt, climbed down a rung, refastened my belt and eased myself away from the mast for a little more space.

"Hurry up," shouted Colin. His arse was twitching and he wasn't laughing this time. I just smiled to myself and carried on snapping in my own time. I climbed down, stepped off the mast and Colin said to me, "You took your fucking time," in an admonishing sort of way to show he was boss. The C.I.D. detective stepped between us, smiled at me and held his hand out for the camera.

"They'll be long gone by now," he said, loud enough for Colin to hear, and winked at me.

Colin and I drove out first and I caught him giving me a sideways glance. He paused at the kerb, looked right then left, then pulled out slowly, and headed for Dungannon at a sedate thirty to forty miles an hour.

"Can I help you?" asked the police sergeant behind the desk.

"We've come to collect Trevor's personal effects," Colin told the sergeant while holding out his ID. The sergeant looked at us, slightly confused, and tried to work out who Trevor was.

"It's the guy that was shot at Coal Island last night," I explained. A light came on in his eyes and he disappeared into the back. The clip of his shoes bounded off the hard wooden floor and bare magnolia walls, and echoed around the featureless, soulless, furnitureless station. Colin and I didn't speak. We just waited. Neither of us was in the mood for conversation. Before the noise of his shoes had died away it struck up again as he began his return. The sergeant appeared with a large clear plastic bag and placed it on the counter slightly to the right of us. A pool of Trevor's blood had seeped out of his clothing and it now lay congealed at the bottom of the bag.

The sergeant spoke with an emotionless, matter of fact and slightly calloused voice. He sounded as though this was a weekly non-event. He reached into the plastic bag, withdrew a smaller plastic bag then consulted a check-list.

"One wallet," he said, reaching into the small plastic bag. He withdrew the wallet and placed it on the counter in front of us, then ticked it off his check list. He dipped in again, drew another item out and held it up. "One Saint Christopher medallion," he said. The medallion spun on the end of its chain and a thin shaft of sunlight filled with floating dust sparkled upon it. It was the only ray of sunshine in this drab, dreary and dreadful place.

"Didn't do him much good, did it?" he said, placing it on the counter and ticking it off. He ran through the items as though in robot mode: extract, name the item, then tick it off. He finished ticking the items in the small plastic bag, then reached into the large plastic bag for Trevor's jacket. His hand came out so fast I thought he'd been bitten by a snake. His top lip curled up slightly as he raised his blood-stained hand and looked at it.

"Back in a minute," he said, spinning on his heel and disappearing into the back again. It was slightly longer before he returned this time, but the clip of his shoes still hung in the air from when he'd departed. He glanced at the large plastic bag a couple of times and he knew that we knew that what was coming next was not procedure, but continued anyway.

"The large bag only contains items of clothing. Could you sign here?" he said, pushing the checklist towards us. He placed the checklist between us, then held out a pen to us, not knowing who was in charge, so that either of us could sign. He just wanted to get the fucking ordeal over. Colin signed and I picked up the bag, then we left.

Hardly a word passed between us on the way back. We were lost in our own worlds, and numb. I cannot remember a single second of that journey. We just departed, and arrived.

We climbed out of the car at HQ and went to its boot. I reached into the boot, pulled out the large plastic bag and fished the smaller bag out of it. I gave the small bag to Colin and he headed for the door of HQ while I jumped into the driver's seat. Colin turned when he got to the door. He realized that I wasn't with him and came over to me.

"Where are you going?" he asked. "To dispose of Trevor's clothing," I replied.

Colin hesitated. Thought about it. Then left me to it. I drove down to the car park which was in front of Wheels's office and parked, lifted the bag out of the boot and walked across the square. I knew that if I handed Trevor's clothing in it would sit dormant on some lonely shelf somewhere, waiting for someone to make a decision on what to do with it. It was soaked in Trevor's life blood and I didn't want that.

I headed for a rusty, lidless side-punctured fifty-gallon oil drum that stood in a corner of the car park that was used for burning classified waste. I stopped off at a skip, climbed up its side, leaned in and gathered some newspaper and some wood. I piled the wood onto the top of single screwed-up pages of newspaper and sobbed. The sobs were so big my chest heaved involuntarily and my body shook. That small chink of ice in my chest that had appeared at the beginning of my tour had now become an iceberg. The iceberg had become so real that I could physically feel it banging against the sides of my chest as I sobbed. It bobbed up and down as though floating in Antartica. I didn't think I could swallow any more bitter pills, but they still went down. The iceberg couldn't get any larger, but the intensity of the coldness of it grew. It leapt into my throat and I was having serious problems breathing. I gulped, then gulped again and just managed to force it down. I lit a long taper of news-paper, waited until it was aflame, then dropped it into the drum. Assisted by the breeze blowing through the punctured sides, the dry wood quickly caught. The fire took on a life of its own and I had to step back because it was giving off so much heat. I picked up a piece of wood, then hung Trevor's jumper from the end of it and introduced it to the flames. The flames diminished and retreated, as though slightly afraid of the jumper. They licked it, tasted it, decided they liked it and then they grew larger. They sprang into life, danced more vibrantly and became brightly colourful. The flames devoured the jumper and converted it to nothingness. Trevor's body was now nothingness, his soul

159

elsewhere. I went through his clothes, one by one. Then came the last item, his jacket. I hung it from the end of the stick and gave it to the flames. The flames backed off and diminished and I was in danger of losing the life of the fire. I lifted the jacket up and gave the fire a chance to come back to life. The flames knew they would have to work hard on the blood-soaked jacket, but they didn't know whether they could cope with it. They became small. They became deep blue. They licked and sampled what was on offer, realized they could cope and sprang into life once more. I looked up. I said a prayer and forced the prayer into Heaven, hoping that Trevor would receive it. I wished him all the best.

I rubbed my chest again and hoped that the iceberg would melt. I heaved and the iceberg moved upwards. I felt sure that I could shriek and gob it out. I imagined it being expelled from my throat and crashing down onto the tarmac and shattering on impact where it would explode into a thousand splinters which would lie there for ever, too cold and intense to melt. I was aware of a presence and I turned. Ray was standing there. I didn't know how long he had been there. I certainly didn't hear him approaching. We didn't speak – we just stood there, staring at the all engulfing flames. I didn't even know he'd gone until the flames devoured the last threads of Trevor's jacket. Then I turned and he wasn't there. Had he been there?

The house had a quiet feel to it as I parked the car in the drive, an empty unlived feel. Dave, a neighbour of ours, called me as I got out of the car. He came over. "Jean and Anna-Lisa are over at our house. What happened?"

"One of our lads got shot this morning. It was Trevor."

"So that's it. Jean wouldn't tell us anything. I looked out of the window and saw her wandering up and down the road in a daze. She's in bits. She's still at our place," he said again, "Do you want to come over?"

"Thanks."

Anna-Lisa came to greet me when I went into Dave's house, so I picked her up, then went and sat next to Jean on the settee. She'd been crying for a while and I could still feel the lingering spasmodic tremulous sobs going through her.

"Come on Jean, let's go home," I said to her, rising off the settee and waiting for her to follow.

"Thanks Dave," I said as we left.

Our house was stone dead when we entered. It was as though nobody had lived there for years. The spirits and atmosphere that we had introduced and imparted had vanished in one foul swoop, as though a blast of cold air had swept through and cleansed the place. It was time to move on. We were not welcome here any more. I introduced noise into the house by switching on the radio and made Jean a cup of coffee laced with brandy. The heavy atmosphere lifted slightly as the day wore on, but it never fully recovered. The three of us went walking in the late afternoon to escape the house that was no longer our home. We returned only when it was dark and we were exhausted.

We could hear the phone ringing as we approached the house, but neither of us was in a hurry to answer it. We just plodded on. Whoever was calling was persistent. The phone rang, and rang, and rang. When we entered, the ring seemed to take over the whole house, as if it was a living thing crying out in pain. It seemed to force its way into my ears and intensify. It was an unlawful intrusion and I mentally ignored it, strolled over unhurriedly, and answered.

"Hello." There was no immediate answer from the other end and a flash of anger passed through me. I continued to hold the phone next to my ear and waited for the anger to subside, then I said, "If you don't answer in the next five seconds, I'm going to hang up"

"Is that you Dad?" said Belinda. "I've been trying to get through to you all day." The lines must have been chocker again as relatives of those serving in Northern Ireland checked on their loved ones. The relatives would have felt relief that they were safe after they had talked, then sorrow as they knew some other mother, wife, son or daughter would get no answer.

"I was really worried this time, Dad," said Belinda. "The news said that a rigger had been shot."

"Your dear old Dad is still here," I told her. "You'll have to put up with me for a few years yet." I continued reassuring her that everything was fine, then said, "Your mum needs cheering up. I'll put her on." Jean had stood next to me through the whole conversation with suppressed excitement. She kept holding her hand out for the phone when she thought our conversation would finish, then she would withdraw it as the conversation continued. Jean brightened up immediately as she began to natter to Belinda, so I left them to it. Anna-Lisa couldn't miss an opportunity to speak to her mum, so she was next.

"Fancy a chinkie tonight?" I asked Jean as she took the phone off Anna-Lisa, replaced it and came over to me smiling. "Order what you like," I said, passing the menu over. Jean became totally immersed in the menu, and while she was reading it I got Anna-Lisa ready for bed. I walked down the stairs with Anna on my back and entered the living room.

"Have you decided yet?" I asked her.

'Yes. I think I'll go for this beef dish," she said, holding up the menu and pointing to an item on it.

"What number is it?" I asked. She looked up and smiled at me then said, "On second thoughts, I'll go for the prawns." She'd had half an hour to decide what she wanted, and had then changed it, as women do. What would we do without them!

None of us had eaten properly all day and we tore into the food, only now realizing how hungry we were. We licked our fingers and slurped wine and really enjoyed it. Anna-Lisa could stay up until she fell asleep tonight. We weren't bothered. We stayed up until we could no longer keep our eyes open, then dragged our physically exhausted bodies and weary minds to bed, longing for the new day of tomorrow.

"Did you hear what happened over the weekend?" Brian asked me when I got in on Monday morning.

"No."

"The boss went round to see Trevor's wife to offer his help and support, and she told him to fuck off and slammed the door in his face."

I wasn't going to say anything at this moment with regards to the circumstances surrounding Trevor's death, as I assumed an inquiry would take place. If it did, I was never questioned. I received a letter two years after Trevor's death, it read:

(TREVOR'S WIFE) V MINISTRY OF DEFENCE

1. This office deals with litigation cases whereby personnel claim compensation against the MOD. We are at present investigating the above Plaintiff's claim arising from the fatal shooting of her husband, who was killed by terrorists whilst climbing a radio mast at RUC Coalisland.

2. As it is believed that you were serving with Trevor's unit at the time of his death, it is requested that you contact this office and speak to the case investigator, Warrant Officer Class Two Sharon Michael. Please feel free to make a reverse charge call.

3. Your assistance in this matter would be appreciated.

I phoned Sharon and she asked me to forward a report to her on how I viewed the incident. I did. I told the truth. I hope Trevor's wife got her compensation.

We were asked if we wanted to attend Trevor's funeral. I declined. I knew I wouldn't be able to hold myself together.

Paul YoS was leaving this weekend and his replacement had arrived. He was a brusque, moustachioed northerner called Keith who had known Trevor from a previous tour. The two of them had been good friends and Keith had offered to write Trevor's obituary for the Royal Signals magazine, *The Wire*. A couple of days before the funeral I walked into Keith's office and he held out a piece of paper.

"Trevor's obituary," he said. "Let me know what you think?"

I started to read it and couldn't hold back any longer. I found myself an empty office and cried. I had to report in sick. The coldness in my chest was overwhelming me and taking over my life. I picked up my medical documents the next morning from our clerk and went sick. There was a queue there, but I didn't have to wait; the sister ushered me in to the doctor as soon as I arrived.

"Good morning doctor," I greeted him.

"Good morning. What can I do for you?" he asked.

"I've got this strange feeling in my chest," I told him. "It feels like a lump of ice. It started off very small, but seems to keep on growing." I felt my presence in the room, but my presence was not inside myself. I was definitely talking, but my voice was coming from the other side of the room. The doctor shrivelled. He diminished. He shrank into his chair and looked down. We would not make eye contact again. Looking back, I knew what he knew. I was losing it. He recognized the lava bombs spitting out of me and he knew I could erupt at any moment.

"What would you like me to do?" he asked, still looking down. I was surprised at the way he was treating me. Wasn't he supposed to show an interest?

"I'd like an X-ray," I told him from the other side of the room. He wrote out an X-ray chit and passed it over to me without looking up. I left, thinking what a strange man.

I walked into Mushgrave hospital, handed my pistol over to the receptionist and then presented the X-ray chit to him. The receptionist had been quite bubbly to begin with, but after reading the chit he spoke in a very quiet and deferential manner.

"Please take a seat," he said, pointing to some chairs on the other side of room and immediately breaking eye contact. The receptionist picked up the phone, dialled a number and whispered into the handset with his back to me. When he had finished the conversation he turned around, looked down and replaced the phone. Then he sat down and lowered his head to concentrate on some paperwork. Not once did he acknowledge my presence or inform me what was going on. I was feeling strangely alienated. A white coat appeared at a door that led down a corridor. There was an attractive thirty-something brunette beneath the coat and she beckoned me by raising her right arm, holding it out straight in the direction of the corridor and inclining her head slightly. I stood up, walked towards her and before I could draw level with her she was walking down the corridor. I trailed behind and followed a mild-scented perfume towards the X-ray lab. She reached down, turned the handle on the door, stepped inside the room and held the door open for me, while once again beckoning me forward with her arm raised and her head inclined. There were two male X-ray technicians in the room in a rather odd pose. They were stood with their arms folded, leaning against a wall and slightly inclined towards each other. They were having a chat about nothing and there was no reason why they should be in the room. They looked up and nodded, then they looked away and carried on their non-existent conversation. The door closed behind me and the white jacket walked past me and pointed towards an X-ray machine. My thoughts were that she was going through a separation and that she had a man-hate campaign going at the moment. I tried to lighten the atmosphere with small chit-chat, but got no feedback, just nods.

"If you'd like to wait in reception for half an hour, I'll let you know the results," she said when she'd finished. So you can speak, I thought! I looked up when the corridor door opened. I watched the white coat with nothing inside it walk towards me. She stopped five feet away from me. She leaned forwards and tried to keep her distance from me as though I had some communicable disease and proffered my X-rays to me.

"Your chest is clear," she said. She then spun on her heel and quickly disappeared. I withdrew my weapon and left. I felt very lonely. Very alone.

12

THE WIND DOWN!

We were torn apart by the third death in the Royal Signals, especially as it came from within our small compact unit and that most of us had known all three. The healing was very slow. We needed something to lift us. Christmas was coming and along with it the mess dinner. Brian was now flying everywhere finalizing the last-minute details and double-checking everything. Transport would pick us up and drop us off. All we had to do was have a good time.

Brian had played many a joke on me. Tonight was my night. I drove in with Jean, wanting to get there early so I could set it up. When we arrived, there was a problem. To prevent anyone outside The Unit seeing our real names, the seating plan was not on display. The problem was I didn't know where Brian was sitting. I'd been waiting a long time for this and I was going to be robbed at the eleventh hour. We went into the bar and ordered drinks.

"You're early!" shouted Robbie Wheels from the door.

"Just thought we'd get a drink in before the rush," I answered.

"Good," he said. "I was supposed to stay and watch the seating plan. But I'm not quite ready. Could you look after it while I go and finish?" "Sure. Bring it over," I said, not believing my luck.

Not many people had known Brian's second name and it had taken me ages to find it out. I'd approached the admin staff first. They were so tight-lipped I felt like a spy. "Ask Brian," they'd said. I finally wheedled it out of his best mate, but had to tell him why. I looked at the seating plan and it was the usual table arrangement in the form of a U. The bottom of the U was classed as the top table where the upper ranks and honoured guests sat. Down each leg the ranks reduced, ending with the youngest sergeants in promotion terms. Stuck on the end of one leg was the sergeant last promoted; he was Mister Vice and responsible for striking a small wooden hammer on a gavel. It captured everyone's attention and was followed by proposing the toasts. I stood next to Brian's chair while Jean fished around inside her bag. She pulled the items out, placed them on the table and glanced furtively around. I picked up the black cotton and reeled off five lengths. Jean began cutting small strips of sellotape and handed them to me one by one. I taped one end of the cotton onto the underside of each piece of cutlery. Then I fed the cotton over the edge of the table. Jean was still giving furtive glances; I had to laugh.

"We'll get banned from the mess if we're caught," I told her. She took it seriously. Couldn't see the funny side.

"I'm staying for two more minutes, then I'm going," she said. It made me laugh even more. Which made things worse.

"One minute left," she said, blowing down her nose and placing one hand on her hip to show her annoyance. I ran my hand along the edge of the table and gathered the threads stuck to cutlery on the right-hand side. I twisted them together and sellotaped them to the right front leg of Brian's chair. I then gathered the threads from the left-hand side cutlery and sellotaped them to the other front leg of Brian's chair. I stood behind the chair and checked it out. The threads were practically invisible against the dark brown polished table and dimmed lighting. Happy, I picked up the seating plan and went back to the bar, just as the first guests arrived.

There were a huge variety of mess kits, which depicted the regiments The Unit was drawn from. Most were the same style. The distinctions came in the colour: a red jacket with black cuffs and black lapel; the reverse colour with black jacket and red cuffs and lapel; green jacket and black lapels; black jacket and yellow cuffs and lapels. Some wore waistcoats with a gold chain strung across the pockets. Some had epaulettes and some had lots of medals. There was one common factor, the black dickie bow.

Trousers were all the same, black. The difference here was the stripe running down the outside of each leg. The stripes were different colours. Long hair, short hair, built-up-on-top hair or let-it-hang-down hair. The women looked relaxed and radiant. Their eyes twinkled gaily and their perfume wafted across the room. They flirted, laughed and smiled, cascaded feelings normally hidden on this thankless, dreary tour. Their dresses were an array of colours, shapes and materials. Their boobs edged over necklines and pouted teasingly. It was a heady cocktail.

The gong gonged over the buzz of conversation and the laughter died. A hush descended.

"Dinner is served," said the Mess Manager.

The old warriors and honoured guests of the top table led us in. They stood behind their chairs and waited for us to settle. Silence reigned. Grace was said. A loud 'Amen' came from the diners, then the scrape of chairs across carpet could be heard. I wasn't going to miss it and stood watching. He stood with one hand on the back of his chair, talking to the lady on his left. She had an extra low-cut dress on and was sat down. He could have been there all night. I was the only one still standing apart from Brian, and Jean was becoming concerned.

"Sit down," she said, tugging at my jacket. I ignored her. He was moving the chair, still talking and looking down. CLANG. Brian was riveted to the spot, trying to work out what had happened as a quiet hush settled around him and people stared. I sat down and practically wet myself. He reached down to pick up the cutlery. Must have felt the thread. It clicked.

"*Rigger*," he shouted, looking round for me.

The people around Brian were in stitches as he explained. Then a slow Mexican laugh washed around the tables as they passed it on to the person next to them and so on. The food was excellent and the wine flowed. The problem was you weren't allowed to leave the table until the speeches were finished. Mister Vice was Stuart Clerk. He'd been recently promoted and was on his first mess dinner. Robbie Wheels was next to him (poor Stuart). Robbie had managed to get a bottle of wine off one of the waiters. He hid it under his chair and pulled it out whenever Stuart's glass was half empty. Three-quarters of the way through dinner Stuart was bursting.

"There's no problem going to the toilet," Robbie told him. "We all do it. Crawl under the table and disappear through the curtains on the left."

There was no problem crawling out and no problem crawling in. There was a problem when he got back though. I can still remember the innocent inquiring look on his face as he knelt on the carpet and rested his chin on the table.

"Where's my chair?" he asked.

Robbie was all for leaving him. The girls weren't. Stuart got his chair back.

The tables had to be cleared of everything before the toast could be made. It was only when there was absolutely nothing on the table that Stuart realized.

"Where's my hammer and gavel?" he begged and pleaded. Brian stood up and called, "Mister Vice."

Stuart looked around helpless, reluctant to stand. It wasn't until a slight impatience went round the room that Robbie let up. He pulled the hammer from his inside pocket and the gavel from under his cummerbund and placed them in front of Stuart. Stuart physically sighed. He stood up, struck the gavel and announced, "The Queen."

Everybody stood up and repeated, "The Queen."

The diners sat down amid the clatter of glasses. Then it was coffee, After Eights and liqueurs with a cigar or cigarette. The boss thanked everybody for their hard work and support. Then it was retire to the bar while the band set up. Our stomachs were still awash with food and wine when the band beckoned us back in. It was too soon. We carried on talking, drinking and circulating, letting our stomachs settle, then slipped in to the ballroom. It was drink more, laugh more and boogie the night away. Jean knew it was my time to go when I leaned back to take a drink. One minute I was leaning back on my stool, the next I was lying on the floor looking up at the Garrison RSM, my head between his feet. He looked sternly down and frowned, trying to look serious, but it was no good. I'd got the giggles. The more he frowned the more

169

I giggled. I couldn't get up I was giggling so much. Someone had to do something. I was helpless. Tutting and annoyed, Jean grabbed my arm, dragged me up and helped me on to a mini-bus.

A call came from South Det on Monday saying there was a fault on the intercom and could I sort it. It was just what I didn't want. I drove down, still tired and fuzzy-headed from the weekend, hoping it would be easy; it was. There were empty bunks everywhere with people on leave and I couldn't see why they should go to waste. I came out two hours later. I yawned, stood on the step and stretched. I scraped my hairy teeth with my furry tongue and smacked my lips together, then headed for the brew point. Bill Spanner was there and we chattered on about what we were doing for Christmas. I was looking round the cars when he told me about a bit of a fright he'd had last week.

"Oh yeah, what happened?"

"Well, I was working on one of the operator's cars. It was a wiring fault and the underside of the dash had to come off. Guess what dropped out?" I looked at him but he held it back.

"Go on," I said.

"A snake. Apparently it had been lost for a couple of days, and there it was under the dashboard."

"What are you looking for, Jack?"

"Where's the pursuit car Bill?"

"You haven't heard then?"

"No."

"They rolled it first time out and totalled it."

I was just not with it. Bill was coming out with some crackers and I was only half taking it in. Time to go. Two miles outside Lisburn I heard it. A terrific explosion. I wondered who'd copped it this time. The way I was coming in took me past the married patches and it was a hive of activity with all the emergency services in attendance. The IRA had left a car bomb close to the perimeter fence of camp. There were no casualties as the area had been cleared and fortunately there was enough spare housing capacity to re-house them all, but what a Christmas present!

The next night was the Sergeants' Mess Christmas Draw. All the Senior NCOs who'd had their houses blown up were there, determined to carry on. The organizing committee had hung an electronic sign over the stage, one of those that you can type into and it comes out in the form of moving writing. It kept us updated on who'd won prizes. Some humourous messages came later:

Cheap house for sale – minor bomb damage – Apply Ray Tech.
Rooms to rent – cheap rates.
Houses blown up for free – apply IRA.

It was hectic with all the parties, but we'd managed them. A four-day rest and tonight it was ours. Some of the lads had asked Jean to make an extra-strong dish of something and she was busy putting the finishing touches to a chilli.

"Try this?" she said. It nearly blew my head off.

We were busy all day, non-stop till five o' clock. We stood peering round the kitchen, checking the creation and making sure we hadn't forgotten anything. Jean looked at me and smiled.

"Fancy a drink?" I asked.

We sat on the settee with our feet on the coffee table, sipping a glass of wine.

"Here's to our next posting," I said, chinking glasses.

"I'll drink to that. I never thought it would come," she said.

Brad was first to arrive with Wendy, followed ten minutes later by Brian and his wife.

"Where can I leave this?" asked Brian, holding his Browning.

"I've set a bedroom to one side. I've got a key," I told him.

I was on my way down when the bell went again. For the next half-hour it was up down up down, stowing coats and weapons. The party was bubbling with Jean plying the punch and I was met by a hail of verbal when I got in there. They were ahead and I needed to catch up. Three punches later I was with them, taunting, teasing and laughing.

"What about charades?" I asked. The girls were all for it, the men shied away, as usual. I split them into two teams, getting on with it and not giving them a choice. Wendy and I were always taunting each other, so I dragged her up.

"I'll supply the first one, then each team that wins supplies the other team with one." I pulled Wendy close,

"Alien," I whispered.

"It's a film – One word," shouted her team. She lay three fingers across her arm. "Three syllables," someone said. First syllable she mimed, pointing one finger in the air. She squeezed a thumb and finger nearly together. "It, and, the, to." "A", somebody shouted and Wendy pointed. "Alien," somebody else shouted.

I couldn't believe it. Right out of the blue, just like that. Up yours, she said with her eyes and stuck her nose in the air. A couple of mimes later they started to get involved. They were taking it quite seriously, wanting to win. Not too seriously, there were plenty of ridiculous shouts, which got everybody laughing. The men were now fighting for their turn and it was hilarious. Ray got the Concise Oxford English Dictionary and blew it. That was Wendy's doing. Everybody seemed to be on form with brilliant repartee. Jean's head popped around the kitchen door.

"Food's ready," she shouted.

"All right. Just one more then we eat," I said.

"Wendy, you're not getting away with it that easy. Come here."

She came over with that 'I can crack anything you give me' look on her face.

"Donald Duck," I whispered. She paused for all of two seconds, then smiled and winked at me. "It's a book and a film – Two words – Second word," her team chanted. She pulled on her ear for the sounds like sign. She pointed to Ray and started thrusting her hips backwards and forwards. The clues were close, but nobody wanted to say that word. Shag – screw – bonk came out. It had to be Brian,

"Fuck," he shouted. It went quiet. Then Wendy started pointing to him, jumping up and down and there was uproar. She pulled on her ear again and pointed to Brian.

"Fuck – duck." Wendy was leaping for joy.

"Donald Duck!" shouted Brad.

She went over, gave him a kiss then turned and gave me the one finger. They didn't need telling twice. It was now a mass exodus to the kitchen.

There was chilli, quiche, homemade coleslaw, sausage rolls,

172

sandwiches, chunks of pineapple and onions and cheese on sticks, bowls full of salad, and fresh cream gateau. The garlic bread came out of the oven and they were dipping in before Jean had removed the foil. They blew on their fingers and ouched, then burnt them again as they went for more. Boy, were they hungry! Jean stood back, flabbergasted, with a big stupid grin on her face. She was delighted.

"Jean, what's in this?" said Ray, with sweat pouring off his forehead, pointing to the chilli.

"Is it too strong?" she asked, now looking all concerned and thinking she'd overdone it.

"No, it's brilliant. Try this lads, it's great," he said, pointing his finger at his bowl of chilli. They dipped in and gasped. But instead of backing off they grabbed a plate and dished up. They were laughing and joking, fanning their mouths and blowing out at the same time. Some even stood outside in the zero temperature to cool off. It was the first dish to disappear and Jean had been worried about it all day.

It was getting on for one before guests started to leave. They apologized. "Baby-sitters," they said, not really wanting to go.

The smell of gun oil overpowered perfume in the darkened hall. It was quickly followed by the sound of weapons being cocked, safeties being applied and the scrape of metal on leather as holstering took place. By two we had the place to ourselves and sat there reminiscing. Sipping a last coffee, we were exhausted. The pots would wait till tomorrow.

I came home elated from my first day at work in the New Year. There were four packing cases in the boot. Before going to pick up Belinda, I screwed a couple of boxes together, just couldn't resist it. Belinda wanted me to pick her up at nine and I was feeling a little carefree when we made the arrangements. I'd been on a high all day and had to remind myself that practically all deaths occurred at the beginning or end of tours. The IRA knew you were inexperienced when you arrived and on a high just before you left. They selected those times to target you. Most regiments were given an arrival and departure present. Bubbles of excitement kept overwhelming me every time I thought of leaving this god-forsaken place. I had to keep calming myself and concentrating, as I had done for the past twenty-two months. It wasn't easy and it took presence of mind. I kept reminding myself – Del in his last week, Dave in his first week and Trevor in his first few months.

I picked Belinda up and she was bubbling.

"What's got into you today?" I asked.

"I'll tell you and mum together when we get home," she said.

She paced the living room, happy and alive, waiting for us to sit. Couldn't contain herself any longer and spurted it out.

"Rob leaves in a couple of weeks and the house has been finalized. So we can go together," she said, with a huge smile on her face.

"Well there's only one thing for it," I said in a serious voice.

"What's that?" asked Belinda, slightly concerned.

"I'm going round to the off-licence for a couple of bottles of bubbly."

We toasted Belinda, Rob and Anna-Lisa when I got back, then sat around chattering incessantly. My new posting in, less than two months to push and now this good news. The boxes trickled into the garage and were slowly and happily filled. The car had to be left on the driveway. It was double-checked every morning for suspect devices, even though we were inside the wire. The under-side of the car plus the wheel arches had to be checked as some devices were triggered by movement and were attached to the car by means of a magnet. Other devices were placed under a wheel and responded to pressure. Whatever device it was, it would have been found. I went over the car with a fine tooth-comb every morning, determined to get away in one piece.

An urgent job came up where an antenna and transmitter had to be provided and it had to be done tonight. It was Ray and I again. The last job we would do together, and it was deep in bandit country. Neither of us had visited this location so we carefully studied the map and the out of bounds situation. The nights were now long, cold and dark, which was a big plus on the climbing side. Snow had also been forecast and we wanted to get there before it fell. It would be dark and the area was sparsely populated; we deemed the early start okay. The climb would probably be left until

174

the early hours. We planned, logged and tested everything. We then knocked off and got our heads down for the afternoon.

We met at seven. We'd be there by nine. We set off in the Hiace and had been travelling for about an hour when it came – an endless procession of frozen water globules dripping from a rent in a cloud. The snow had arrived early and was coming down in heavy giant flakes that soon carpeted the whole area, giving a picture of quiet serenity as snow does. The giant flakes mesmerized you if you allowed it. They came towards us, stuck to the windscreen and momentarily obscured our view, until they were flicked away by the whip of a wiper. The headlights carved a white turbulent tunnel through them. We drove down it, heading relentlessly on.

Four miles from the location Ray was taking the snow into account by driving slowly. A car was sitting on our tail, unable to overtake due to the weather. It was happy just to follow. Three miles later, with one mile to go, the one car behind had become three. We formed a small convoy, drawn together by weather conditions. The fact was we were all heading in the same direction. We represented togetherness and total anonymity. We passed through a smattering of houses. We knew exactly where we were. It was up a hill and down, then we were there.

We started to climb and then it happened: the wheels lost traction and spun. I wanted to keep the momentum going, so before the van actually stopped I was out and pushing from the back. We were just moving, but only just. The warm self-contained cocooned tin capsules behind that had formed the convoy seemed to have no problems with traction and slowly pulled out and passed. Their drivers or their passengers, or sometimes both, stared at us while wriggling in their seats as one involuntarily does while observing someone else's discomfort. The convoy was no more. The last car passed. We were alone, glad of it and thankful there had been no offers of help.

We were struggling in a hostile area, trying to reach a safe haven just over the hill and it wasn't working. The van had come to a complete halt. I wanted to discuss the situation, so I walked up the side of the van, opened the passenger door and said, "What do you reckon Ray?"

"How about reversing down the hill and having another go?" he suggested.

"I'll watch you back," I said. To prevent our accents being over-heard we decided to communicate by one bang on the side of the van for stop and two for go.

One bang. He stopped. There was a car coming up the hill, so I stood and waited. The car's lights illuminated the whole area, casting moving shadows as it pulled out and overtook. The passenger stared and wriggled. It reminded me of a television set, staring through her window. Which one of us was the programme? We looked at each other. Neither of us knew who the other was, just two people passing in the night, never to see each other again. It was a typical scene on a night like this. It could be seen enacted all over the country. Two bangs and the van moved backwards, down the hill and along the flat, far enough back for another bash.

We set off with tension in our bodies, trying to force the wheels to grip through sheer will power. I told Ray that if I had to jump out and push again to wait for me at the top if the van picked up speed and I couldn't catch it. It was at about the same spot that it lost grip again. I was out at the back and pushing again. Trillions of giant flakes followed the last trillion. We both knew that if we didn't make it this time we wouldn't make it all. The van was just inching along. Probably four spins of a wheel to two inches of forward travel. Ray played with the clutch, trying to prevent wheel spin, marginally succeeding. I had my back against the rear doors and my hands under the bumper. I was thrusting down with all my might onto the two biggest muscles in my body, trying to make the van move. Covered in snow, with snow falling, you'd have had problems seeing me. But you would have seen the great lungfuls of hot breath spewing out, condensing and forming a moving drifting cloud above me. The hot breath cloud was bathed in the dull red glow of the rear lights. That unreal feeling crept in again. Straight-backed and head back I pushed harder. I could feel the cold from the door creeping its way into my body as I strained and willed the van to move. My muscles started to cry out in pain as I forced them beyond their accepted norm, but I wasn't giving up with fifty yards to push. My mind was thinking ahead, trying to work out what we would do if we didn't make it. We could turn around and head back to Lisburn, but we would only get stuck again. It would be a long time before Wheels came along with their four-wheel drive to pull us out, that's if they were able to with the worsening conditions. There would be no point in putting their lives at risk. There was only one option if we had to abandon. Park the van and walk to the location. There was forty yards to go and I was breathing so deeply that the cold air was being dragged to the bottom of my lungs. The air hit the bottom of my lungs like a sledge-hammer just pulled out of deep freeze.

Light burst all around as a vehicle came over the top of the hill and down towards us. It was now darker where I was. Darker because the van cast a huge shadow behind it from the oncoming vehicle's lights. The shadow moved slightly to my right as the vehicle approached, then it stopped. He shouted, the Irishman, trying to make himself heard over the engine revs, asking Ray if he wanted a tow. I couldn't see, but could imagine. Ray would have shaken his head, not wanting his Brit accent detected. The strong Irish accent was louder this time, pressing for an answer. The van moved no faster than an officer pulling out his wallet, and that is slug slow. I was bustin' a gut pushing, heaving and snorting, trying to move this van. The front of the other vehicle came into view. I recognized its familiar square shape. The Land Rover probably belonged to a local farmer. It crunched into reverse and moved slowly backwards, out of view. The driver stayed level with Ray. He was too persistent with his offer of help and the situation was serious. I heard Ray say, "Yeah," and it was a whole new ball game.

I ran alongside the van while looking ahead. I watched the Land Rover back up the hill. I opened the passenger door and reached in. Ray looked at me,

"I had no choice," he said.

There was no time to talk. I grabbed a support weapon and slipped it under my jacket. I put my right hand in my pocket and gripped it through the lining. No point in advertising. We could still come out all right. I popped all the press studs on my jacket so there was only the zip to release, just in case. I understood perfectly the position Ray had been put in. If he had spoken they would have heard his accent. If he hadn't spoken it would have been just as suspicious. CATCH 22.

The Land Rover was out of sight on the other side of the hill, but we were reminded of its presence. Its headlights shone upwards into the trees, highlighting the snow and the heavily laden branches. He was reversing to a point where he could turn round. Then he'd reverse back to us. The other alternative was that he was going for help and for weapons.

You don't know where it comes from. You're absolutely knackered, but you seem to be able to dredge up superhuman reserves of strength in a potentially tight situation. I put my back against the van and began to push again, heaving, straining, willing and praying. My muscles seemed to be the only part of my body sending messages to my brain and they weren't nice ones. I sensed the van beginning to pick up speed, ever so slowly, but it was there. It faltered slightly and I growled, re-gripped the bumper and pushed harder. How, I don't know, but I did. The wheels began to grip. It moved a touch faster. I wondered if now was the right time to move for the cab, but decided to wait just a little longer. Another touch of speed and I was now in danger of being left behind if I stayed longer. I stood and turned. It started with my shoulders sagging, then my arms hanging limp. A great weariness rippled through my body, leaving me totally spent and bone-weary. I'd had enough. I just wanted to fall into the trees at the side of the road and sleep. My calf muscles felt like lumps of lead hanging from my legs, hard and knotted as though they'd just been attached and were not really part of me. Burning sensations ran up the sinews in the centre of my arms from over-straining. My back ached and my whole body was a heaving, gobbing, heavy wreck.

I stood watching the van go up the hill, its dark shape silhouetted against the white background. The smudge-red rear lights glowed ghoulishly and the blue-grey exhaust cloud rose to melt the oncoming flakes. My mind was everywhere but here. I was looking into wonderland with the peaceful snow plopping around me. Or was it a picture postcard? No, it was News at Ten showing the road conditions. I was everywhere but here. The trees beck-

178

oned once again. I could fall into them for as long as I liked, then wake up fully recovered, in the real world. It was so tempting. It took a conscious effort to break the thought. I realized Ray would stop at the top and wait for me. Why couldn't he just go on and pick me up in the morning?

My body didn't want to do as it was told. I told the legs to run but they dragged. I told my right hand to squeeze the pistol grip but it didn't. I reached down and grabbing hold of the barrel and pushed the weapon back under my jacket. My body had been pushed beyond its limits and was now rebelling by taking command, instead of my brain. It was now dictating the terms. I struggled to gain control, finally won and pushed on. I was running and cursing. The end of the barrel of the support weapon was striking my right knee as it came up. It sent jolts of red hot pain to my brain which were converted into spots of coloured lights bursting before my eyes. Every inch of my body was crying out and I looked at the trees again. They were beckoning and offering sleep and security. I was beginning to feel physically sick as once more I urged my body on. My right hand was trying so hard to keep a grip on the support weapon; it was aching beyond belief. I even thought about stopping and changing hands. Had I done so I would have lost ground. I gritted my teeth and carried on, cursing every time the barrel dug into my knee. Onwards and upwards and for ever a day, whatever that means. But I thought about it while slogging up that hill. Finally reaching out, I opened the door.

Fuck. It still wasn't over. I tried to raise my right leg to get in, but the barrel was digging into my knee. My right foot brushed against the moving wheel directly under the door and I smiled. I even laughed. Ray looked at me as though I was off my trolley. I was. If I let go of the door handle to grab the weapon with my left hand, I could easily slip, then slide under the wheel. Well, wouldn't that be fucking all, I thought, after all this fucking effort the wheel ran over my fucking foot.

FUCKING HELL!!!

While still running and hanging on to the inside door handle, I manoeuvred the weapon over to the centre of my body. It would be a quick movement. Left hand off the door handle and onto weapon, right hand off the weapon and onto the seat. It worked perfectly and I tried to climb in.

FUCKING, FUCKING, FUCKING HELL!

The whole FUCKING world was against me tonight. I tried to bend so I could duck into the van, but I couldn't. My jacket was too well-fitting and when I bent forward the support weapon poked into my chest. I really wanted to FUCKING scream, but held it in. The scream seemed so real. It went round and round inside my skull, bouncing off the sides like some solid object with perpetual motion. On and on for ever and I wondered if I'd actually screamed aloud as Ray glanced over again. He gave me a funny look. Did it fucking matter? NO, IT FUCKING DIDN'T!!!!!

I seemed to be in a world of my own with everything else receding. Ray seemed to be at the end of a tunnel and the engine noise was muffled and distant. All I have to do is fall into the darkness under the trees and I won't be missed. They seemed to be calling out to me, stretching out a hand, offering peace and sanctuary. They were so inviting. What was I fucking doing here pushing this fucking van, taking all this fucking pain? I don't need this crap, I told myself. There was only one real choice. Letting the door close, I dropped back a couple of feet, still being hit in the knee with the barrel. The only difference this time was it was my left knee. I half-unzipped my coat, put my right hand inside, grabbed the support weapon and fished it out. By the time I looked up, the situation had changed yet again. I was running slower or the van was going faster. I didn't know which. It was the first time I'd doubted I'd catch it. I was aware of every cubic inch of muscle in my body. They shrieked and cried at the torment and punishment, but still carried on. One more try. If I don't get it this time, FUCK IT.

My mind was wandering again. I thought of my next posting to Germany. I had to drag it back. Concentrate. I was reaching out for the door handle again. I couldn't believe it when I touched it. Come on, one last effort and you're there. I practically fell in and raised myself onto the seat, closed the door and placed the support weapon across my knees.

The heat in the van reached down into every crevice of my lungs

180

and seared them as I sat gulping air. I was already soaked in sweat, but it got worse. Bucketfuls were pouring out of my body and I felt like a hot, wet, steaming, blubbering mass. I looked up just as the tail lights of the Land Rover peeped over the brow of the hill. They looked so odd, giving off their incandescent glow with hot carbon monoxide rising in between like some belching dragon. Releasing the safety I said, "Go round him, Ray. I can't see any headlights coming."

He pulled out. The van stuttered as it left tracks made by the previous cars and crossed the virgin ridges in between. My guts leapt into my mouth as we lost traction with the change of direction. Every fibre in my body willed it on. We crossed the ridges of snow and fell into the tracks on the other side. We picked up speed again. Ray tooted as we passed the Land Rover. We received a full beam flash from his headlights in acknowledgement. Mr Anonymous probably had no idea an automatic weapon was pointing his way, or the trauma that we'd been through as he sat in his warm cosy cab. But, if he made one wrong move, I would have blown his fucking head off.

It was down hill all the way and the location was in sight. We had a good view of it. This one was different. Instead of the usual high security wall to protect the fragile building, it was the reverse. A strong wire-mesh fence surrounded the bunker-like fortress, allowing the inhabitants to look out and see what was going on. The problem was people could look in. We radioed ahead to other members of The Unit who'd arrived earlier to let them know we were coming. A member of the RUC was making his way from the concrete and steel mass towards us as we approached the gate. He must have been covered from the building and felt safe as he just sauntered across, not a care in the world.

"Park undercover round the back," he said, pointing to the right-hand side of the bunker. Ray obeyed. He drove round the back, picked out a hardened shelter in the headlights and parked under it. It was that one extreme to another again. No security lights and deathly quiet, except for the fall of snow as we stood waiting for our night vision to kick in.

"Where now?" I asked Ray.

"Over here," shouted the policeman waiting in the shadows. We couldn't see him, just headed for the voice. We followed him around the building, then waited while he opened half a door. The door could only be opened half at a time, due to the sheer weight of the two-foot-thick steel it was made of. He only bothered opening the bottom half. We had to duck below the top one.

Whispering ceased as we entered and all eyes were on us. I felt slightly naked as they eyed us up and down. They drew their conclusions, cast us aside and carried on whispered conversations, as though we didn't exist. I scanned the room looking for a familiar face, but didn't recognize anybody. Ten or twelve men in civilian clothes sat around, and it wasn't difficult to tell who they were. They sat amid an array of weapons scattered across the floor, lines of life's experiences etched deep into their faces, a quiet confidence exuding from them. Ray tugged my arm. "This way," he said.

We both followed the policeman along a passage and into a room where the equipment would go.

"I'll leave you to it. If there's anything you need, give me a shout," said the policeman before disappearing.

I told Ray I was going out. "To check things out," I said.

I stood in the shadows, looking up at the one hundred and forty-foot mast. There was room below the top antenna to fix mine. There were only two antennae on the mast. It would be an easy climb. I looked beyond the fence at the surrounding hills, just visible through the snow. This could be dodgy. I was totally exposed from the start. I thought about the Land Rover and the possibilities of him passing on our visit to friends who would have a clear view into the compound. I could leave the climb until early morning, but the sky might clear, or I could do it now with reduced visibility.

I laid the feeder cable out for a smooth uninterrupted climb. I pocketed the tools and spares and stepped into the shadows. I put on my belt, zipped the antenna to it and waited. My jacket rustled as I put my grey, knitted, woolly hat on; then the only sound was snow. I stood for ten minutes, letting the flakes settle on me until I resembled a snowman, then climbed slowly, trying not to draw attention. I slithered up the mast like a snake hunting its prey and belted off below the top antenna. Then, with creeping movements, so as not to dislodge the snow, I reached for the nuts and clamps in my top pocket. I began attaching the antenna, working unhurriedly, efficiently and methodically. Long gone were the days when fear crept in. They had been replaced by a total awareness of the situation, the need to get things done, first time and right. My hands passed through the numb stage and onto the glowing stage. Gloves would have been a hindrance. I attached the antenna and moved slowly down. It was too risky to hang one leg over the upper cross-member and work with no belt on the snow-covered mast, so I belted off each time I stopped. I zipped the feeder cable to the mast leg, unbelted, moved on and re-belted. It probably took an hour to climb up and down, but it seemed like minutes I was concentrating so hard. On the ground, I reached up to the steel catenary wire that ran from the mast to the equipment room. I zipped the feeder to it and along it and finally pushed the end of the cable through the access duct. Ray came into the equipment room with two coffees and said, "What do you reckon?" Meaning can an antenna be attached and if so when.

"I've done it," I said.

"*What!*" he said incredulously. "I thought we were going to be here all night." Then, "Mind you, we could be here for days if the weather doesn't improve." I sipped my coffee, lit a fag and watched Ray fix the equipment to the wall, solder a connector on to the end of the feeder cable and test. It was done.

"Let's have a look outside," said Ray.

The weather had changed dramatically. There was now just the odd snowflake and it was warmer. I glanced down to see where I was walking and noticed Ray's footprints where he'd trodden and compressed the snow. It was melting.

"What do reckon? It seems to be clearing up," I asked.

"I'm all for going back as soon as possible," he said.

"Let's give it another half-hour, then decide," I said.

We checked again, and it was definitely thawing. The roads would be even clearer than the compound with the passage of cars. We decided to head back. There were absolutely no problems on the way back. The snow was turning to slush on the minor roads, and the motorway was practically clear with the gritting. We off-loaded the stores, parked the van and jumped into our cars. I'd volunteered to hand in the weapons and book in. Ray went home. The duty Bleep was in the control room along with Colin and Keith YoS. They were pondering over a map and talking as I booked in.

"How did it go?" asked Colin. I just *exploded*.

"What the fuck's it got to do with you?" I shouted with my hands tightly clenched and my arms forced down ridgely. There was a tight ball at the back of my neck and the ice lump in my chest glowed hot and cold. I can clearly remember the droplets of spittle coming from my mouth and landing on them. All my pent-up feelings poured out and splattered over them like acid being added to water.

"I can't stand people who sit at fucking desks all day," I ranted. It was a weird experience. I was now two people. 'I' was totally calm inside. I listened to this other me outside. I shouted and raved and gave them shit. They both stepped back from the unexpected onslaught, mouths falling open in complete surprise and staying there. I spun round and left, not giving them a chance to reply. Walking toward the door I was actually laughing inside, laughing at this outer person who had just given them shit.

"Well done you other me," I thought, chuckling to myself. I calmed on the way home. I analysed the two-person experience I'd gone through and I came up with a conclusion. I was losing it.

The house was deathly quiet, but I couldn't go to bed yet. My brain was operating in the megahertz range with all sorts of random thoughts popping up. Full, real life coloured detailed visions of sections of the evening flashed up right before my eyes in cinemascope and 3D. I couldn't shake them. I poured a stiff one, followed by two more. They helped the visions to fade. I began to wind down. Probably two more and sleep was a possibility. I showered. Finally I crept into bed. No matter how quiet I was, Jean always woke.

"Everything all right?" she asked.

"Sure," I replied. "Just need some sleep." It was a long time in coming.

Two weeks to push and was I happy. Colin came into my office and announced, "Your replacement has been delayed by three weeks," then started laughing. I joined in. I told him his wind-up wouldn't work. His face became deadly serious. He repeated it.

"Well that's fucking tough. I'm going on the original date," I said and walked out.

We'd been living in a practically empty quarter for the past three weeks and he expected me to do it for an additional two. If Manning and Records couldn't get there fucking act together; tough. The flight had been booked. The removals were coming in ten days. Belinda and Anna-Lisa had already returned to the Mainland. Jean was going back once the furniture had been collected. I would follow two days later. I had that foreboding feeling. I was overstaying my welcome (Welcome! Definitely the wrong word). All the lads wanted to work with me. I'd been practically everywhere, and always come back. That buoyant feeling of knowing everything would be all right and I'd always return had gone.

Colin kept telling me I would have to stay those extra three weeks, so one day I leaned over and put my nose one inch away from his. I remember him pulling away with his face screwed up as my foul-smelling tobacco-laden breath entered his nostrils. I followed him, looked him in the eye.

"Fucking charge me. I'm going," I said.

He got the message.

My farewell piss-up was not what it should have been due to the circumstances. The lads I'd worked closely with took me out and tried to get me pissed. The drink didn't affect me one bit. I remained totally sober, and totally hostile. I FELT LIKE RIPPING SOME FUCKER'S HEAD OFF.

I flew out the next day.

EPILOGUE

I, like many another squaddie, left Northern Ireland a bitter and angry man. The experience has changed me forever. I can never return to the person I was and I don't want to. The fear was real. The comradeship, the stress, the long hours and never being able to relax anywhere, anytime, was a normal day. There was an emotional turbulence at not being able to retaliate when your mates were picked off, but then who would you retaliate against? You just had to soldier on and gulp down the bitter pills. It started just after Del and Dave were murdered at the IRA funeral, my first week in the Province. A small chink of ice, roughly the size of an ice cube suddenly appeared in my chest. It was as though I'd undergone surgery and an implant had been inserted. The small cube of ice had a life of its own and it grew and grew until finally, just before I left Northern Ireland, it filled the whole of my chest.

I became unpredictable. Anyone treading on my toes would face a full verbal onslaught.

Everybody is affected in one way or another by their tour over there, including the wives. It can sometimes take years for the infestation to appear. Then a mental breakdown occurs. The soldier diving for cover every time he hears a loud bang! The wife who cannot stop peering through the curtains every time a car stops outside! One way or another, it affects you. It changes your mental attitude to life. It can give you moral fibre and a whole new meaning to life, if you come out of it alright. Go to Kings Cross or other seedy areas of London and you'll find him there, the exsquaddie who hasn't come to terms with it, it is preventing him from returning to society because of his hostility and he doesn't know how to overcome it, or the fact that he is doing it. It seems a normal day to him.

It happens so often when you are demobilised from The Forces. You are thrust together with your partner that you have spent so much time away from and you realise that you don't get on.

I left the three bedroom detached house that I had spent so much time making into a loving home and became homeless and unemployed. My daughter Belinda said that I could move in with her while her husband was on a six month unaccompanied tour of Cyprus but I would have to find somewhere to live when he came home. I became a nanny to my two grandchildren who I dressed, made sure they ate their breakfast, got them to school, then I came home and did the washing, ironing and cut the lawn while still firing off my CV. My CV finally worked and I was offered a job in London just before my son-in-law came home. I moved into a bed-sit in London and a new adventure in my life began. Neasden, Hampstead and Richmond in bed-sits with shared toilet and bathroom is not something I expected at the age of forty- nine, but there I was. After twelve months in bedsits I contacted the Royal British Legion and told them of my plight. They offered me a two bedroom flat in West London at reasonable rates so I took it. My contract in London ran out after two years and I was once again cast into the sea of the unemployed so I decided to write a book, this book, while continuing my search for employment.

Twelve months! It was the longest period of unemployment in my life and I didn't seem to be able to shake it. I had applied for any job that I felt that I could do but the answer was always no. But looking back it seems as though it was meant to be that way and I would not be offered a job until my release came. My weekday routine continued with the walk, breakfast and bash away at my book and now I worked harder and longer as the final page loomed. I became more intense and it had an odd effect on me, whenever someone spoke my fingers would twitch as though gliding across the keyboard and the words they had spoken would then appear on an invisible screen above their heads.

A constant surge of excitement buzzed around my body as the book drew to a close, and something very very extraordinary was waiting for me. The last page, the last sentence, the last dot of a full stop appeared and then it happened. The coldness in my chest, that iceberg that had been with me since my two year tour of Northern Ireland suddenly erupted and an overwhelming torrent of overheated anguish, or was it anger, gushed upwards from my chest, restricted my throat and avalanched out of my mouth with a force and intensity that shocked me. That anguish! That cold super heated anguish that I had carried with me for so many years splashed onto my legs like boiling water and scalded them. The heat had been so intense that I lowered my trousers and fully expected to find blisters, there wasn't any, but there were large red blotches. My body shuddered as I fell onto the bed and I curled up into the fetal position as huge wrenching sobs raked it. The healing process had begun and warmness began to seep into my chest, I could feel the mental and physical changes taking place within me. It wasn't until that moment that I realised how enormous that burden had been and it took two days, two whole days for that boiling anguish to pour out, and only then did the sobbing ease. Had that festering coldness remained inside me I would probably have become a bitter and twisted old man.

MOVING ON

The phone rang a week later, 'A high tech company is looking for a trainer, are you interested?' enquired the agency.

I knew nothing about robotics, but I had been out of work for twelve months. Do I turn it down?

'The first course starts in six weeks,' said the MD. 'Here's the manual,' which was the thickest manual I had ever seen.

Six weeks at extremely good rates, deliver the first one week course and that'll be it I thought. Travelling one hundred miles to work was not something I wanted to do everyday so I found a house share and stayed over night during the week. For the next six weeks I sat with my nose in the manual and played with a robot. I was taking in so much information that my brain was on permanent overload and when someone asked me a question the information (if I knew it) would burst out of my mouth so fast that it would splash over the person asking and make them step backwards. Then I would think, 'What did I say?'

Two years later I told Sue, my partner that I couldn't go on commuting like this and that I was going to look for work in London or move nearer to the job I had.

'I've been in London for twenty years,' she told me. 'I'm coming with you,' so I rented a three-bedroomed semi and we moved in. Eighteen months later we moved into our new four-bedroom detached and finally got married.